BREAK FREE

Praise for *Break Free*

'I met Sabari because I was meant to meet her. I lost my father very suddenly, and it left me with many unresolved feelings. What happened in the next couple of sessions with Sabari is something I might not have recognized then but I live it today… The belief and joy of always finding music in the noise. Healing is one of the most beautiful and forever-evolving journeys because it is filled with endless possibilities and the ability to rise above the chaos and find light. *Break Free* is an important and relevant book in our fractured times when many of us might be looking for healing and guidance to rise above the dissonance.'
—**Aditi Rao Hydari, actor and dancer**

'Sabari's strong voice will gently lift you with the wisdom of your eternal lives and the spirit world. *Break Free* is non-negotiable reading for those determined to live powerful, joyful lives on earth. Your consciousness will never be the same again.'—**Anupamaa Dayal, designer, columnist, healer**

'A gentle beginners' guide to therapy and healing. *Break Free* is a powerhouse of information and ideas. A sturdy lamp of a book for anyone setting out on a journey of self-discovery or simply curious about it. A must read.'—**Anuraadha Tiwari, writer, filmmaker and light worker**

'In leadership and in life, we often focus on the visible—performance, outcomes, results. But the invisible forces within us shape so much of how we show up. *Break Free* offers a timely reminder that the answers we seek are often buried within. Sabari's work invites us to pause, reflect and courageously explore the patterns that hold us back. This is not just a book; it's a roadmap for personal transformation.'
—**Sanjay Gupta, president, Asia-Pacific, Google**

BREAK FREE

HEAL YOUR PAST, EMPOWER YOUR PRESENT

Sabari Chakraborty

HARPER
NON-FICTION

First published in India by Harper Non-Fiction 2025
An imprint of HarperCollins *Publishers*
HarperCollins *Publishers* India, Cyber City, Building 10-A,
Gurugram, Haryana-122002, India
www.harpercollins.co.in

2 4 6 8 10 9 7 5 3 1

Copyright © Sabari Chakraborty 2025
Illustrations by Sripana Chhetri

P-ISBN: 978-93-6989-199-3
E-ISBN: 978-93-6989-151-1

The views and opinions expressed in this book are the author's own and the facts are as reported by her, and the publishers are not in any way liable for the same. Some names and identifying details have been changed to protect the privacy of individuals. None of the content in this book is intended to be a substitute for professional medical advice and should not be relied on as health or medical advice, diagnosis or treatment. Always seek the guidance of your doctor or other qualified health professional with any questions you may have regarding your health or a medical condition.

Sabari Chakraborty asserts the moral right
to be identified as the author of this work.

All rights reserved. No part of this publication may be reproduced, stored in a retrieval system, or transmitted, in any form or by any means, electronic, mechanical, photocopying, recording or otherwise, without the prior permission of the publishers.

Without limiting the exclusive rights of any author, contributor or the publisher of this publication, any unauthorized use of this publication to train generative artificial intelligence (AI) technologies is expressly prohibited. HarperCollins also exercise their rights under Article 4(3) of the Digital Single Market Directive 2019/790 and expressly reserve this publication from the text and data-mining exception.

Typeset in 11.5/15 Sabon LT Std
by HarperCollins *Publishers* India Pvt. Ltd

Printed and bound at
Thomson Press (India) Ltd

This book is produced from independently certified FSC® paper
to ensure responsible forest management.

HarperCollins Publishers, Macken House, 39/40 Mayor Street Upper,
Dublin 1, D01 C9W8, Ireland

To

*My husband, Indranil (IC), who is the wind
beneath my wings.*

*My four-legged children—Zara, Zen and Tara—who
help me receive and give unconditional love.*

*All the brave energy and light workers out there who
spread their light and help others heal.*

*The courageous souls who embraced healing
and transformed themselves.*

Disclaimer

The contents of this book are intended for informational purposes only and intended as an aid to spiritual and personal development. The author shares personal experiences, beliefs, and perspectives on past life regression healing. However, this book does not under any circumstance claim to provide medical, psychological, or professional therapeutic advice, or that the techniques mentioned herein constitute a cure for any disease, condition or disability. The contents of this book should not be used as a substitute for medical diagnosis, treatment, or therapy provided by licensed professionals. If you are experiencing any physical, mental, or emotional health concerns, you are strongly advised to consult a qualified medical or mental health professional.

The author and publisher make no warranty regarding the effectiveness, accuracy, or outcomes of any information or techniques discussed in this book. Any decisions you make based on the content of this book are entirely at your own discretion and risk.

The author and publisher disclaim any liability for any direct, indirect, incidental, or consequential damages arising from the use or interpretation of the material presented. By reading this book, you acknowledge and accept that past life regression is a deeply personal and subjective experience, and you are responsible for your own well-being and choices.

Contents

Preface xiii

1. Connecting Your Body, Mind and Soul 1

2. Identifying the Problem and Making First Contact with a Therapist/Healer 17

3. How to Cleanse Your Aura 38

4. Inner Child Therapy: Healing Childhood Traumas That Get Carried into Adulthood 60

5. Going Deeper into the Subconscious Mind 87

6. Regressing to Past Lives 102

7. Shadow Work and the Shadow Self 130

8. Life Between Lives Therapy 150

9. Assimilating All the Concepts, Therapeutic
   Modes and Healing   182

10. Self-Help Tools and Reading List   196

    Masks   209
    Acknowledgements   211

Preface

> 'We are not human beings having a spiritual experience; we are spiritual beings having a human experience.'
> —Pierre Teilhard de Chardin

A few of us might resonate with the above quote conceptually and philosophically, but how many of us acknowledge every day that we are spiritual beings having a human experience? Between amazing and awful, between the mundane and the exceptional, between grief and healing lies the spectrum of living.

Every soul that takes residence in a human body comes with a purpose, and our whole lives go in finding and defining that purpose. Many a time we falter, lose our path and purpose and find ourselves slipping down that rabbit hole of hopelessness and despair. Unable to cope, we yearn for a guide, a mentor, a confidant, someone who understands our 'state'.

Break Free is meant to be a guide to channel the business of living through a prism of healing light and knowledge, enabling you to find a method in the madness. Esoteric concepts of the complex universe we inhabit are introduced and disseminated gently for easy comprehension. This book seeks to illuminate your mind and help you open the doors and windows of your soul to embrace positive change—to learn to let go of deeply ingrained traumas and give yourself a chance to be the best that you can be. The case studies in this book, which are the heartfelt stories of many of my clients, might inspire you to break free from your own sufferings and connect with your soul light within. The more you have the courage to heal, the stronger will you feel the luminescence of your inner light, reminding you that you indeed are a spiritual being, a being of light having a human experience, and that you have seen heaven, earth and everything in between. You are without beginning or end.

Like Lord Shiva, you have destroyed, created, nurtured, annihilated, again and again rebirthed and renewed yourself. An earthly incarnation gives you instant amnesia of who you really are because on earth, we have lessons to learn and karmas to be resolved. However, it is also important to acknowledge that you are infinite, and *Break Free* is your step-by-step aid to remembering just that—your boundlessness.

In the Hindu pantheon, Lord Shiva is known as 'the Destroyer' within the Trimurti, the trinity that includes Lord Brahma (the Creator) and Lord Vishnu (the Preserver). In Shaivism, Shiva is one of the supreme beings who creates, protects and transforms the universe. However, Lord Shiva is also the greatest healer of all. While most people look upon Lord Dhanvantari (an incarnation of Lord Vishnu) as the deity of Ayurveda and the ideal doctor, in the oldest Rigveda, it is Rudra/Soma—Lord Shiva himself—who is the supreme doctor or vaidya. There is a temple near Madurai called Vaitheeswaran Koil, where Lord Shiva is the vaidya and Ma Parvati is his assistant, who nurses souls back to good health.

Shiva is also known as Mrityunjaya, the one who eases the passage to our physical death. Praying to him alleviates our diseases and sorrows. Shiva is the Adiguru of yoga and prana, the very breath that keeps us alive. However, in the universal order of things, before healing there needs to be the dance of destruction, what the sacred texts call tandava, to make way for healing and clearing, thus leading to the resurrection of a new world order.

To embrace this renewal, one first needs to accept and acknowledge the churning of the mind, body and soul. Churning is the indicator that a change is required to calm the waves. In constant churning, there has to be a complete meltdown, after which can begin the restoration of tranquillity and composure.

This theme of resurrection is seen in the mythology of many ancient civilizations, which have highlighted destruction followed by creation, death followed by reincarnation. For example, in Greek mythology, the mythical bird the phoenix experiences cycles of death and rebirth, falling and rising again and again. Associated with the sun, a phoenix obtains new life by arising from the ashes of its predecessor. Philosophers and writers like Herodotus, Lucan, Pliny the Elder, Pope Clement I, Ovid and Isidore of Seville have written and popularized the phoenix motif. When we say 'rise like a phoenix', it indicates a renewal after destruction.

Hindu mythology talks of a decisive event known as the Samudra Manthan, the churning of the celestial ocean, for the divine nectar, or amrita, which will ensure immortality for the gods, or devas. Even the fallen gods, or asuras, wanted the amrita, so they decided to help the devas in the churning of the ocean to get this celestial nectar of immortality. What happened once the nectar was milked out of the ocean is another story, which I would encourage you to read if you do not know it already.

I am directing your attention to this mythological story because the word 'churning' here is very important. Our ancient seers and sages were wise beings, and mythological stories symbolically carry their wisdom for us lesser mortals to reflect on and learn from. They emphasized a churning that would give the gods their much-coveted immortality. Metaphorically, the churning symbolizes going through hardship, pain and danger, overcoming it, reaching a state of blisshood and finally receiving blessings.

In plain speak, it means having the strength and willingness to overcome dis-balance and find balance and harmony.

I am a tweaker of consciousness and a facilitator of soul songs. I am a healer.

There ... I said it.

For fifteen long years, I avoided using the word 'healer' whenever people asked me my profession because it just seemed too egotistical to even utter the word. So I said, 'I am a regression therapist who works with the subconscious mind. I regress people to the roots of their blocks—physical, mental and emotional.' Technically, this is what I still do, but that doesn't begin to describe the results of what I do. For that, healing is perhaps a better word.

In the summer of 2013, a well-known surgeon from a reputed hospital in Mumbai came to see me. Despite having a healthy lifestyle and exercising for two hours at the gym every day, he had to have four stents placed for blockages in his heart. Being a medical doctor and having a good understanding of how the human body functions, he was concerned that despite maintaining an active and healthy lifestyle, he had developed blockages in his coronary arteries.

As we delved deep into his subconscious mind to get to the root of this 'dis-ease', the surgeon went back to his early childhood, where verbal abuse and a lack of love from his parents saddled his heart with deep pain and fear. Throughout his life, he felt this lack of love, and finally, in his early fifties, his physical heart manifested a dysfunction.

Because of the mind–body connection, he understood that this physical dysfunction was rooted in an emotional dysfunction, so no amount of healthy living could keep this disease at bay. As we worked with the wounded inner child and integrated the healing back into the adult, the surgeon's perspective towards his own suffering and towards his abusive parents changed. He could forgive them and free himself of their judgements. Once free of this baggage, he went on to have a pain-free perspective on his own existence, and consequently he now leads a more harmonious, happier life from within.

Amruta, a dentist by profession, came to see me in 2014. For years she had been dealing with a fear of eating food that was not cooked at home. She avoided eating at restaurants and always claimed she was fasting for one god or another when invited to a party or a get-together. But when she met me, she was to get married in a couple of months, and as a new bride, she would have to be part of many celebrations where it would be required that she eat food outside her home. Traumatized at that thought and having no clue what to do, she came looking for help.

Working with her subconscious mind, I guided Amruta to the first time she had felt this fear of eating food outside her home. She went back to a past life as a young woman, in which she was poisoned, along with others, at a big feast organized by a vengeful member of her extended family. The poison caused her a very painful death.

Our body-mind tends to carry cellular memories of trauma as well as of creative gifts and talents. Modern science has proven that our cells contain DNA, which is the blueprint of our complex physical bodies. However, our cells also hold the blueprint of our emotional, mental and spiritual experiences. Our cells remember all that we have been in past lives and all that has happened in this life right up to the present day.

As stated in a BBC report: 'Twenty years ago, an enormous scientific effort revealed that the human genome contains 20,000 protein-coding genes, but they account for just 2% of our DNA. The rest was written off as junk—but we are now realising it has a crucial role to play.'[1] For those of you who are interested in knowing more about what was once called 'junk' DNA, there are quite a few ongoing research findings available online.

Mystics say that all of us are the distilled essence of our collective past experiences, and the cellular memories of all those experiences are very much alive, especially when a trigger is pressed.

Amruta too carried the cellular memories of a sudden and horrific death when she was trustingly eating food at a family gathering outside her home in that past lifetime. So every time there was an occasion when she needed to eat outside of her home, especially after she

---

[1] David Cox, 'The mystery of the human genome's dark matter', BBC, 13 April 2023, https://www.bbc.com/future/article/20230412-the-mystery-of-the-human-genomes-dark-matter.

entered her late teens, her fear of pain and death was triggered subconsciously and she would have a panic attack. We neutralized her fears from that particular past life and healed the cellular memories of trauma.

A fortnight later, Amruta called me excitedly from a restaurant. She was with a friend and, after many years, she had just ordered a dosa and was comfortable eating outside of her home! I was grinning from ear to ear; her voice told me she was too.

These are just two instances out of hundreds of cases, but how else can I describe the above outcomes except to say that they were able to *heal* from their trauma? That is why I think the best way to describe the work I do is by saying, 'I help people heal themselves,' because healing is the ability to connect to an awareness greater than one's regular self, and any person who facilitates that journey is a 'healer', without any attachments to the ego-self. A healer is a conduit who also holds sacred space for others.

This book is a collection of multiple healing situations, and as you read them, I hope you will be able to get an awareness of how, when you wish to, with the help of a healer or through self-healing, you can access the vast power of your subconscious mind and deal with the various blocks that are stopping you from becoming the awesome human being you really are.

Every case in this book is a true account of people who chose healing and empowered themselves to rise above their afflictions. My clients are my teachers, never mind who they are—rich people or poor people, big Bollywood movie stars or hardworking homemakers, light workers or energy healers, well-known conglomerate heads or office clerks, brilliant academics or sweet kindergarten teachers, service people from the armed forces, police personnel, people of science—they all taught me invaluable lessons in healing.

This book is like a healer's diary because it is not only an account of my journey as a healer/therapist, but it is also the account of a multitude of people who reached out to me to help them initiate their own healing journeys. I firmly believe that all of us have a healer inside ourselves. That voice of intuition from our higher selves helps us acknowledge problems, reach out for resolution and finally resolve life-blocking issues, whatever they may be.

Jesus of Nazareth said: 'And you will know the truth, and the truth will set you free' (John 8:32, New Testament). Once we can look truth in the eye, accept it and operate from there, the truth does set us free. I would rather fight for truth than against it. Covering it up also doesn't work because the scale of karma always balances itself. One's own truth can remain submerged in the recesses of the subconscious mind for years and years, but once a catalyst triggers it to burst forth, please have the courage to look it in the eye and do not look away. Many people suffer from depression and anxiety for years, keeping it well-hidden, creating frothy, light-hearted personalities for the outside world. Once the veneer cracks, it is near-impossible to pretend all is well and carry on the same way.

For many, after years of teetering on the edge of the darkest abyss, total annihilation might seem like a tantalizing way out. *It isn't!* We should all aspire to walk out of the shadows into the light.

So step back and seek help. I am a big believer in 'Ask and you shall receive'. Accept your truth, and if it is traumatic and unpalatable, reach out and ask for help.

This book is to remind my readers that you are much wiser than your problems. When drowning in depression, anxiety, defeatist patterns or unhappiness, just make known your pain, and there is always a listening ear and a compassionate hug available. When we seek help, almost always, help reaches us. Help can come in the form of open conversations with close friends and family, or from professional caregivers like doctors, therapists, counsellors, healers, mystics, psychics or shamans. Sometimes it is easier to reach out to professional caregivers as they are objective and trained to help.

Our subconscious minds hold the roots of 'modern memory', which refers to memories from this lifetime, as well as 'primitive memory', which refers to soul memories from past lifetimes. When we can directly work with the roots of any unease or trauma, rather than just attempting to treat the symptoms from the conscious mind, healing is quicker, more effective and non-temporal. When the roots are uprooted, the malaise is cleared.

So when in torment—emotional, mental or physical—reach out for help because stress and sadness need not be a permanent condition in your life. You are here to manifest your dreams, raise your vibrations positively and live your life to the fullest.

My role has been to hold sacred space for my clients, to give them tools and techniques for trauma release and to guide them into the light from darkness. In my clinic, I have watched the magic unfold—big and small—and seen clients' faces glow visibly when the healing has percolated down through every layer of their consciousness. A lot of my clients have kept in touch with me over the years, and it is exhilarating to know that they avoided slipping back into old defeatist patterns and that they have taken charge of their lives positively.

In this book, I have talked about various therapeutic interventions in simple language so that everyone can understand the concepts easily. I have outlined various healing modalities with examples of real-life cases to elucidate the tremendous possibilities of change to which we are all entitled. I have also presented some metaphysical concepts of life and death and of life after death. These concepts have been experienced firsthand by hundreds of my clients. So this is their story as well as mine.

True healing comes from surrender and letting go of control. I allowed *Break Free* to reveal itself to me, to flow, guided by higher beings of light, and I now bring it to you.

I have attempted to present the cases without any judgement and have written about them as they unfolded. Do keep an open mind when you read them and allow concepts, known and unknown, to connect you to the deepest parts of your being. Sit with the questions; the answers will follow.

I release this book into the universe with a lot of love and blessings to you, my readers. Go on, *break free* and give yourselves permission to unshackle from anything and everything that holds you back from being a powerful, energetic being!

Chapter 1

Connecting Your Body, Mind and Soul

'Your body is an absolute mirror of your mind.
As you worry, your body shows it.
As you love, your body shows it.
As you are overwhelmed, your body shows it.
As you are angry, your body shows it.
Every cell of your body is being allowed
And resisted by how you feel.'

—Esther Hicks

Our emotions are stored in our bodies

On 3 December 2018, I underwent a kidney transplant. All year I had been in and out of hospitals while my kidneys started failing, and finally, I had to be put on dialysis. My husband immediately stepped up and offered to gift me one of his kidneys so I could live a life without dialysis. Long story short, his kidney matched very well with my body and the path to transplant was created. I was one of the lucky ones among millions worldwide who got the gift of a kidney and a second chance at life.

But this kidney failure blindsided me. The decline was rapid, and even the doctors were a bit taken aback by the quick downward trajectory that my kidneys took. Doing the work that I do, I had to get to the metaphysical and emotional roots of this physical issue, knowing full well that it was not just a dis-ease (an absence of ease) in the physical body.

I reached out to my friend and colleague in Denmark, Pernille Lund. Pernille is a psychic and a very good therapist and healer who works with the subconscious mind. Our first session, on Skype, threw up two potent revelations for me. As we go further in this book, I will share these two revelations that helped me kick-start my own healing regarding my kidneys.

In my work with body–mind–soul healing, I have frequently experienced how major emotions are stored in and affect significant body parts. Chinese medicine, Tibetan medicine, Ayurveda and homeopathy recognize this.

As per *Medicine Anthropology Theory*, 'In September 2010, the Government of India officially recognized Tibetan medicine as an "Indian system of medicine", making India the fourth country after China, Bhutan, and Mongolia to recognize Sowa Rigpa (Tibetan: *gso ba rig pa*, "the science of healing") as an integral part of its national health care system.'[1]

Sowa Rigpa understands the connection between the body and the mind. Physical well-being and emotions are intimately connected. Grief, stress, tension, anger, worry, fear and guilt are each associated with a particular organ in the body. So physical organs are not just body parts—they are emotional centres too. Chinese and Tibetan medicines believe emotions that affect the heart include a lack of enthusiasm, restlessness, despair, insomnia and deep unresolved grief.[2]

We have, at some time or another, heard of someone (or even a pet) dying 'of a broken heart', and this is indeed a possibility. An imbalance in the heart causes many life-threatening disorders.

---

[1] Stephan Kloos, 'The recognition of Sowa Rigpa in India: How Tibetan medicine became an Indian medical system', *Medicine Anthropology Theory*, 13 September 2016, https://www.medanthrotheory.org/article/view/4637/6336.

[2] Zi-Juan Zhang, Xin Li, Ya-Xing Cheng, Amatti Jorigori, Dongzhu Renqing, Li-Ping Pan, Meng Mao, Xiao-Qiao Ren, Hui-Hui Zhao, 'The psychosomatic thought of Tibetan medicine and its treatment methods' World Journal of Traditional Chinese Medicine, 1 July 2023, https://www.researchgate.net/publication/369833405_The_psychosomatic_thought_of_Tibetan_medicine_and_its_treatment_methods.

In holistic medicine, it is said that feelings of insecurity, fear, aloofness and isolation can physically affect the performance of the kidneys. Metaphysically, the kidneys trap the energy of fear.

Well, my kidneys happened to trap them too. I had a disturbed childhood in a very dysfunctional family—an alcoholic father with a heart of gold, a moody mother and a bunch of emotionally challenged members in the extended family. My paternal grandparents were my anchor in my early years, but then, when I was around twelve, my grandmother became bedridden after a paralytic attack, which also affected her ability to speak without slurring. My paternal grandma was a fabulous storyteller, but her interesting stories from Indian mythology stopped when she fell ill and, with a working mother, I was largely left alone to do things my way.

Throughout my childhood, I always found ways to overcome my deep-rooted fears of annihilation. I had a few loyal friends, my partners in survival. I danced, played teacher-teacher, directed kiddie plays, tried to learn how to cook and found many other creative ways to skirt adult politics. But the abject fear of abandonment, the fear that if my parents divorced, I would be alone, always lurked deep within. I also had fears about my long-term future because I wasn't a decision-maker yet.

Where would the energy of this fear and isolation go? It would eventually manifest in my body. My parents separated when I turned twelve and then divorced. As a fighter, I fought my inner banshees and outer battles.

However, it seemed as though my kidneys had absorbed my fears all along.

As an adult, I have done extensive healing work on myself with other therapists and on my own as well. I have thrown many heavy suitcases full of angst and grief into the metaphorical sea after giving them resolution, in a bid to travel light. Till my early thirties, I was buffeted by tumultuous winds of flux. Though I am not always sailing on calm seas now, I have learnt how to use healing tools and techniques to help myself remain connected to my inner voice. I believe I have succeeded in my own healing process to a very large extent because I feel different from my tortured younger self.

The body always knows

The body, mind and soul are intrinsic parts of what makes us whole—a complete being. Holistic healing delves into the connection between these three to successfully treat a malady or block that a person might be facing.

It may sound surprising, but our bodies have an innate understanding of when it is imperative to heal. The body speaks through signs and symptoms when it's calling for help.

For example, the body can goad you to seek help by exhibiting insistent, unexplained pain. I have seen many times over that a lot of physical pain is directly linked to emotional pain. When the mind is feeling obstructive negative energy, it also obstructs the flow of energy in the physical body, and the emotional pain transmutes into physical pain.

The way we function is that first, we have a thought. Let me present a scenario.

Thought: 'My mother-in-law is coming for dinner, and she does not like my cooking.' This thought creates an emotional response.

Emotion: A negative feeling in expecting a lecture, snide comments or some unpleasantness. Any emotion creates a charge in the body, either positive or negative. In this case, it is negative.

Charge: The feeling of negativity starts building up, slowly hitting the energy flow in the body and then succumbing to stress as the dinner approaches.

Effect: We have a body, but we are also flowing energy. The human body's energy system is related to its material system. The material system of the human body connects to the different levels of physical structure, like genes, organs, muscles and the entire nervous system.

In contrast, in the energy system, intangible or non-physical forces like emotions, thoughts and feelings mesh with each other. Hence, the living body is a combination of a material system and an energy system, just as shapes and their shadows are inextricably linked.

As negative emotions affect the harmonious energy flow in the body, they throw the body out of sync, and in this scenario, by the time the mother-in-law arrives, the emotion results in a painful, pounding headache. Since the body is the last in this chain of energy, ultimately the emotion will manifest in the body. So the connection between thought-emotion-energy flow-body is omnipresent in our lives.

We are aware mental breakdowns occur when the mind is unable to cope with an overload of stress, anxiety, panic, grief or depression. In such situations, sometimes we seek help, but sometimes we don't. When we don't, we open up the possibility of being overpowered by these disharmonious elements, which affect both our short-term and long-term functioning as a balanced being.

Psychosomatic illness

You might have heard medical practitioners label certain diseases as 'psychosomatic'. This is when emotions (psyche) manifest in the physical body (soma) as a disease. Psychosomatic illness is a situation in which the mind influences the body to create or add to an illness.

Psychosomatic disorders resulting from stress may include hypertension, respiratory ailments, gastrointestinal disturbances, migraine and tension headaches, pelvic pain, impotence, frigidity, dermatitis, ulcers and many more.

When a person is guided to the root of what is causing the mental dis-balance, the physical dis-balance can be treated or managed. While medical doctors should be consulted for the physical symptoms, it's important to visit a psychoanalyst/hypnotherapist or counsellor to find the root of the issue and to have therapeutic intervention for the mind.

Let us take a common medical problem: the migraine.

Migraines do not have a particular medical treatment, so allopathic doctors mostly focus on pain management with painkillers in a bid to reduce the pain, generally with little long-term alleviation of pain. However, when the root cause of a migraine is identified in the subconscious mind and treated, patients get long-term relief from pain and discomfort, and for some, the migraine itself vanishes.

How can I claim this? Simply because I have worked with a lot of severely affected migraine patients over the years. When all else fails, desperate patients turn to alternative therapy, and nine times out of ten, their migraine either completely fades away or is effectively managed without medication, with the help of a few healing tools.

Your body and triggers from your past lives

In the summer of 2012, Janki (name changed on request) from Indore called me, asking for an appointment and to see if I could heal her migraines. I had worked with quite a few clients suffering from migraines, so I told her I would try and help her. Having suffered from terrible migraines for nearly seventeen years, Janki was desperate and agreed to come to Mumbai to see me.

The day of her scheduled appointment, the doorbell rang, and I opened the door to find a woman in her forties standing with a small suitcase, her eyes squeezed shut and face contorted in pain. She looked like she was going to collapse. I quickly held her up, ushered her in, offered her water and just asked her to sit down and breathe deeply. After a while, she composed herself enough to splutter that she was having one of her migraines. She took a pill, and after a while, told me that the painkiller was starting to work and that she was in less pain now.

'Will you manage to do a session today, in this condition?' I asked her with concern.

She propped herself up and nodded. 'I arrived in Mumbai yesterday and stayed with a friend. After this session, I go back on an evening flight, so I have to do it today!'

My mind quickly processed the pros and cons of the situation. Ninety per cent of the time, I have observed in my sessions that the root of a migraine is in a past-life injury that led to physical death. When the trigger is high—in this case, pain—it is like a bridge that enables the therapist to go to the root quickly and work with the client to neutralize it.

However, when there is extreme physical discomfort during the session, the conscious mind is in full control to find ways to deal with the discomfort, and this can stop the person from focusing and connecting with the subconscious mind, where the root lies.

With Janki, time was of the essence, and I had to quickly make up my mind. I decided to do the session and asked for divine guidance so that the outcome would be for Janki's highest good.

As we started the induction to put Janki into a meditative, hypnotic trance, her body looked calm and peaceful, and her eye movements showed me that she was slipping into the hypnotic state effortlessly. I gently guided her to the root of the migraine: When was the first time she had felt this debilitating pain?

Janki went into a past life where she saw herself as a fifteen-year-old girl wearing a salwar kameez and going into a forest to collect twigs and wooden logs to make the kitchen fire. It was somewhere in India.

In the room, suddenly, Janki's body started trembling, and then she started screaming, 'Oh no ... no ... oh no ...' She began to sob.

Through her cries, Janki blurted out that a pack of wild dogs had come out from some bushes and were attacking her. She was trying to escape, but she couldn't, and she fell to the ground as the dogs tore into her. They were biting her face, forehead and ears, and Janki could feel a searing pain in her head and forehead. Then she choked and said she was going to die. She died in that past life from severe head injuries from the attack by the pack of wild dogs.

As I guided the soul out of the body, beyond the physical pain, and eased this transition, Janki's soul-mind hovered on top, looked down and saw the mangled body of a young girl bleeding profusely from the head and forehead, and she felt immense pain and sorrow.

As facilitators of past life regression (PLR) therapy, therapists always need to heal the trauma of that life, rewrite the pain and guide the client to surrender the trauma and move into healing. There are many tools and techniques that PLR therapists use to do this. The most important point is that before the client comes back into their current life consciousness, the root that created pain, suffering and unease in the current life needs to be neutralized. In the timeline of the soul's journey, it needs to become an incident without a negative charge around it.

After Janki surfaced from the session and was fully integrated back into her consciousness and her body, she said she was feeling better and that the pounding pain was gone.

What I had completely forgotten and what surfaced in our post-session talk was this: When Janki called me for an appointment, she had asked fearfully if I had a dog at home.

'Why?' I had asked her in surprise. 'Have you ever been bitten by a dog?'

'No,' she had replied. 'But I always check before going to someone's house because I'm petrified of dogs!'

She made me promise that I would keep my little pug, Zara, in another room while she was in my house. Of course, the terrible fear of dogs now made sense to us both.

Janki looked drained but much calmer when we parted. She said she would be in touch.

Three months later, she phoned to refer someone to me for therapy. She sounded light and breezy, and eventually I asked how her migraine was these days. After a short silence, she said, 'Oh, that!' She no longer suffered from searing migraine pain. Sometimes her head would feel slightly heavy, but when she used the meditation techniques I had taught her, the heaviness went away. (The pain-relief meditation is at the end of this chapter.) I was so happy hearing that her seventeen years of severe suffering were over. But I completely forgot to ask her if she still has a phobia of dogs!

Migraines, as I have seen, tend to have roots in a past life, where the soul died from terrible physical pain. The cellular memories of that severe pain can get triggered in subsequent lifetimes as well.

Below is an account of another client of mine who suffered from migraines:

'Pain became a habit for me because having a migraine was a part of my life ever since I was a child.

Gradually and painfully, I learnt to live with it. I tried medicines of various kinds. Relief happened in short spells, but migraines didn't leave me.

'One day I was meeting my old friend Sabari, whom I hadn't met for a while. The afternoon was wonderful. While catching up, she asked me about my migraine, and I replied that it still troubled me and that I didn't know when I would be able to live without migraine attacks. That's when Sabari suggested that going to the root cause of the migraine might help, and she promised to hold my hand through it if I had any fears or apprehensions about exploring the root. It was hard for me to believe that a non-cognitive, non-medical intervention would bid my migraine adieu.

'But nothing was working and I was suffering, so I wanted to give this healing a shot. I began my sessions with her. It was tough. The inhibition to completely surrender was indeed a journey. In one of my regression sessions, I saw myself being struck on the head and experiencing excruciating pain lifetimes ago. I was a young Roman soldier on a battlefield, fighting, when an axe came down on my head and split it open. I died in excruciating pain. That pain was brought forward in my present life. With Sabari's guidance, I was able to see and close that past-life episode, healing my cellular memories of deep pain. It's been seven years now. I don't have migraines anymore. I do have minor headaches occasionally, but no painful migraines that require hiding in a dark room, feeling sick to the core.

'I am truly grateful to Sabari for helping me overcome my challenges.'

—*Tamara Nedungadi, fifty-six years old, filmmaker and educator*

In dealing with different cases over the years, I have also seen that asthma, allergies, psoriasis and various recurrent skin conditions have unresolved past-life roots.

Countless clients have passed through my clinic looking for a solution to a medical problem that modern medicine was unable to treat and have found the cause of the physical problem rooted in a mental and psychological dysfunction. When they were guided to the root of that mental-psychological dysfunction, they were able to feel much better.

Manas

In the Vedas and other Hindu scriptures, the mind is known as manas. Manas is not understood the same way the mind is in modern science. In Hinduism, manas acts like a receptacle for the senses, where memories, perceptions and emotions are stored and used by the higher mind to make decisions and make sense of the world. The subconscious mind is this 'manas', which holds the holograms and roots of our emotions, perceptions and mental/emotional memories from all our past lives.

A part of the subconscious mind holds all perceptions and memories from this life, known as 'modern memories'. The subconscious mind also holds all our past-life memories and the learnings and emotions connected to them. Similarly, these are called 'primitive memories'. Another deep part of our manas is the superconscious mind, a space that holds 'soul memories', or memories of us as energy beings in our real home, our soul home up there in the spirit world. I talk about the superconscious mind in detail in the Life Between Lives chapter. We are a complex yet effortless combination of all these memories affecting our bodies and emotions.

In this chapter, I have given an overview of how the body–mind–soul connection works for us sentient beings. However, illnesses are also karmic—which we will discuss in detail later in the book—and a huge teaching tool for learning lessons in our soul journeys. We choose challenging medical conditions because through them, we finish assimilating and resolving difficult life lessons and transcend to a place of higher awareness.

Meditation for pain relief and release

- Sit comfortably or lie down and allow your eyes to close gently.
- Relax your body, and inhale and exhale deeply, 12–15 times.
- Breathe in through the nose and exhale through the mouth.

- With each inhalation and exhalation, relax your body and mind.
- Visualize and feel that from an unknown source high above you, there is a sparkling stream of bright white light falling all around you. Connect with the light and feel its brightness and warmth surround you.
- Now connect with any pain or discomfort in the physical body and allow it to be released into this sparkling white light surrounding you. When you are surrendering the pain or discomfort into the white light, you might feel it leaving you like molecules of black/grey dust or vapour. Let it go. The more you surrender, the lighter the physical body will feel and the brighter the light around you. Soak in the light, feel the warmth penetrating all the cells in your body as each cell opens up like a little flower. Let the warmth go deep into you.
- Visualize and feel that the bright white healing light is now forming a cocoon all around you and you are pain-free and relaxed in this cocoon of light. Seal the energy of this lightness and the brightness of the white light through every layer of your consciousness.
- When ready, count yourself up to integrate back into your physical body without any physical pain. Count from 1 to 10 slowly, silently, and whenever you are ready, open your eyes gently.

Chapter 2

Identifying the Problem and Making First Contact with a Therapist/Healer

> *'I think the hardest part to get to is that point of asking for help or reaching out to other people and being honest with yourself.'*
> —Mary-Kate Olsen

The first step in your healing journey

Making a choice to ask for help is the biggest step towards self-empowerment. The first call to a therapist can be a difficult one. For many, it might feel like it's coming from a space of personal failure. But for some, it may also feel empowering to have accepted their issues and be open to looking for a resolution.

The first contact I have with clients is usually through a phone call or an email. Along with logistical information, the reason for seeking help is briefly discussed and I also let them know how I work with the subconscious mind and how they might benefit. If everything resonates with the to-be client, we set up the first session.

The first session forms the bedrock of all future therapeutic interventions. This is the session when the therapist/healer and client establish a rapport, and the therapist listens indepth to the presenting problem of the client.

However, language is man-made, and beyond a certain point, the subconscious mind cannot process only spoken words. Writing is an activity of the subconscious mind, so we tend to express ourselves better in writing rather than through speech. When we pen down difficult emotions or overwhelming feelings, we feel lighter because it creates a catharsis from deep within.

In the same fashion, art and sketches are products of the subconscious mind. The subconscious also gives us a lot of potent information through non-verbal cues—postures, expressions, nervous tics, hand movements, etc. A great book to read about this is *Peoplewatching: The Desmond Morris Guide to Body Language* by Desmond Morris.

The first session with a client is all about subconscious information, joining the dots for the client and me. Understanding client expectations and the therapist's grasp of the presenting problem is crucial so one is not beating around the bush but going straight to the crux of the issue.

To add one more layer to my understanding, I use all the tools available to me as a healer—reading between the lines, non-verbal cues, mentally underlining oft-repeated words, seeing the aura and the energy signature radiating from it and finally asking the client to draw or sketch with coloured crayons. In the early years of my practice, I learnt metaphor therapy from a really good teacher, Kirti Bakshi, in Mumbai. She is a metaphor therapy specialist, and over the years, I too added my own layers to this knowledge and honed it into to a beautiful tool to access and read the subconscious mind, going beyond spoken language.

Chetan Roy, an ex Wall Street banker and financial strategist, who is now giving back to society in various ways, shares his story about his incredible path to healing. From hopelessness to hope, in his own words:

'I first met Sabari at her beautiful home in Goa a year after my divorce. It was 2015. My marriage had been extremely traumatic, and the divorce had been painful and difficult. I felt that Sabari's form of subconscious-mind therapy could help me cleanse emotionally. It would perhaps help me shed the kind of self-limiting emotional baggage that many of us carry for years.

'I will admit that I wasn't quite sure what to expect, not having done this form of therapy ever before. Sabari made me comfortable and explained the process to me, and we got started with me being provided with an A4-size sheet of white paper, coloured crayons and instructions to draw anything I liked. It took some time, but after a bit of effort, I freed up my artistic self and drew an elaborate picture.

'What Sabari did next blew me away. She looked at the drawing and proceeded to describe my inner psyche in a way known only to me. My fears, my inclinations, my passions, my personality. To this day, I remember the feeling of incredulousness as I kept hearing her describe me to me. I felt like I was hearing a mirror. Not looking into but hearing a mirror that was integrating the various thoughts and observations I had had over the years into a singular coherent narrative. I was hearing the inner life of this person who was me from someone who barely knew me or anything about me. And it was all completely, unnervingly accurate!'

That first meeting set the bedrock for Chetan's healing and put both of us in a nonjudgemental comfort zone with each other. It is important that the client feels comfortable to fully open up and trust the therapist with issues that might never have been discussed with anyone else in their lives before.

In India, we say, 'When the shishya (disciple) is ready, the guru appears.' I believe when a soul is ready to shed unwanted baggage and be free, the right healer appears.

Chetan worked with some issues of angst and forgiveness connected with his marriage and his acrimonious divorce and was able to reach a beautiful place of grace, where he was able to let go of his old baggage and feel free. However, I sensed there was still quite a bit of emotional debris deep down that needed clearing. Being a busy banker, Chetan had come to Goa only for the weekend, so we did not have time for more sessions during that trip of his. I gave him some tips and healing techniques to manage his emotional life and Chetan left feeling reasonably lighter.

A few years later, Chetan fell seriously ill. The doctors took nearly five months to diagnose his illness, and what began as a cough and cold turned into an attack of pleurisy, or water in the lungs. Along with allopathic doctors, he met homeopathic doctors as well, in a bid to cure his undiagnosed illness. An acupuncturist who treated him for a while told him that it was very clear to her that his illness was rooted in unresolved grief, possibly from the emotional trauma of his marriage and his divorce, or the sudden illness and death of his mother just before his marriage. These three life-changing events had happened in quick succession along with a host of other serious life issues, including his father's sudden and premature demise just a few years before all of this—and it was possible that the emotional build-up had contributed to damaging his health. He had accumulated over two litres of fluid in his right lung and had become short of breath. The fluid was drained twice by means of a medical procedure, but his lung just kept filling up again.

Chetan finally met an allopathic doctor who was unequivocal about the line of treatment. As he started the treatment, Chetan remembered what the acupuncturist had told him and decided that a visit to me was due.

I had come back to Mumbai by then, after a four-year stay in Goa.

When Chetan walked into my office, he looked frail, having lost a lot of weight, and with his skin emanating that unhealthy look of illness and pain. His aura needed cleansing as his energies were below par and all the complicated medication was draining him.

This is what Chetan had to say about the aura cleansing session:

'I remember that my astral body was covered with some sort of white and dark sticky web or covering, which had to be peeled away. We spent a good part of the first session doing this—cleaning up and removing the film that was preventing my energies from shining. Sabari also added a mantra and a protective practice to my daily meditation.'

I will talk about the aura and aura cleansing in detail in the next chapter. Here I am giving an overview of how healing typically unfolds after a client shares their presenting problem.

A week later, Chetan came for his next session. Here is an account of what he experienced, in his own words:

'The second session was dramatic, to say the least. I remember it vividly even today. It started with me climbing up from a vast, deep well. The well was very high and wide. The top of the well was not visible, and it was easily about ten human beings in diameter. The inner wall was lined with dark grey brick. I was scaling up the brick diagonally, step by step. It was tiring and seemed never-ending. When I finally came out of the well, there was a dense field of plants all around. The field stretched out for as far as I could see. The plants were about my height and obscured my vision. I walked through the tall plants as if I were propelled to do it. I walked faster and faster and eventually broke into a run.

'Suddenly, the field cleared. I was on a hillside. I could see myself, a young boy, running on the hillside. It was a beautiful green, like in the first flush of monsoon in Maharashtra. The sky was filled with large storm clouds. The clouds were dark, sliced by streaks of the setting sun's orange and red. Large swathes of white lightning flashed in the sky. In the background, I could hear one of my favourite devotional songs. It was a song that I often played at that time at home when I lay in bed recouping. The entire scene was filled with the song.

'I ran into the lightning without fear. As I did, it entered me, filling my entire being. I felt the most incredible love ever. I felt like I had touched an inexhaustible ocean of love. I felt that I had been protected all my life. That there never was, nor ever would be, a moment when I was not loved, never a night when I would not be protected. Gratitude welled in my heart. Tears trickled down from my eyes, wetting my cheeks.

'The vision then changed into a temple. A temple with a dark blue sky behind it. There was a trident and a form of Shiva. A small light inside the temple. Awe. Reverence. Peace. Sabari held the space for me and encouraged me throughout this soul journey.'

So what do you think happened here? Why did Chetan's subconscious mind throw up these visuals that he felt deeply in his body, mind and soul?

Energies, frequencies and vibrations

Nikola Tesla, a Serbian-American inventor, electrical engineer and physicist (10 July 1856–7 January 1943), correctly said, 'If you want to find the secrets of the universe, think in terms of energy, frequency and vibrations.' Further back in time, the great bard Shakespeare wrote in his tragedy *Hamlet,* in which

Hamlet tells his friend Horatio, 'There are more things in heaven and earth, Horatio, than are dreamt of in your philosophy.'

What a beautiful combination we are of the body, the mind and the soul. These three affect each other directly and indirectly, in ways unfathomable to the cognitive mind. During healing, besides our physical bodies, our different energy bodies are affected, and higher beings of light connect with our energy bodies to help us heal. This is a very delicate process in which a healer helps the client connect with those healing energies and release all their unwanted baggage into the light.

Chetan's state of mind was beautifully reflected by his subconscious mind through a deep well (a place where anyone might feel trapped), from where he had to haul himself out into the light, yet he was surrounded by tall grass, which obscured his 'vision' (the capacity to delve within and not without). Then 'something' propelled him to fight his way forward, and he actually broke into a run (breaking free), undaunted by flashing lightning, allowing it to pass through him and immediately feeling incredible love filling him up (divine healing energies) and feeling blessed with the knowledge that he is loved and always will be loved.

In cultures worldwide, documented evidence shows that a multitude of people have felt this kind of incredible divine love, which changed their lives forever. Sri Aurobindo, the Indian philosopher and yogi, writes about this kind of experience in *The Synthesis of Yoga*. He wrote:

> 'Influence is more important than example. Influence is not the outward authority of the Teacher over his disciple, but the power of his contact, of his presence, of the nearness of his soul to the soul of another, infusing into it, even though in silence, that which he himself is and possesses. This is the supreme sign of the Master. For the greatest Master is much less a Teacher than a Presence pouring the divine consciousness and its constituting light and power and purity and bliss into all who are receptive around him.'[1]

Paramahansa Yogananda's book *Autobiography of a Yogi* has sold millions of copies worldwide and has been translated into over fifty languages. Yogananda travelled extensively in the West and gave talks all over America, and thousands of people connected with him. Yogananda said it was not unusual for many spiritual seekers to have experienced amazing, incredible emotional and physical healings that awakened and connected them to their true selves. This is called 'energy healing' by spiritual healing practitioners, and it is what Chetan experienced in his session.

---

[1] Sri Aurobindo, *The Synthesis of Yoga*, Incarnate Word, https://incarnateword.in/cwsa/23/the-four-aids#p17-p33.

It was time to go deeper into Chetan's psyche to the roots of pain and dissonance created by his divorce and dysfunctional marriage.

The third session took him to another life. He saw himself as a white man dressed in a suit sitting in an airport in Europe.

Chetan said, 'I am feeling unhappy. My wife, who is sitting with me, is also unhappy.'

They left from the airport together. As the story evolved, there seemed to be a deep misunderstanding between the man and the woman. He had said something in the past, but his wife misunderstood his intentions. Perhaps it was his choice of words, but she refused to change her perspective no matter how much he tried to disentangle her misconceptions.

Thus time passed. They grew old, spending evenings by the setting sun. When once they would hold hands, those hands now just rested side by side, barely touching, cocooned in resentment and silent fury.

I guided Chetan through that particular past life, encouraging him to uncover the important moments of that life. A time came when he was dying. He lay on a white steel bed in a large room with white walls. His entire family was by his side. His children, grandchildren, some others. But she wasn't there. His wife, the woman he loved with all his heart, the woman who never forgave him. He died with the regret that he could not make amends. It was his biggest failure.

As healers, we guide clients not to live with strong regrets from a past life, as resolution is important so that negative cellular memories are not triggered and do not create unease in the current life. Chetan later said:

'Just as I could feel my life ebb from my body, Sabari eased my soul's passage out of my physical body, and soon I saw myself hovering above the room, looking down, still feeling regret. That is when Sabari asked me to go back to the moment of misunderstanding and reframe what I had said to my wife. Change the story. I did that. Suddenly the scene by the setting sun came back, and the man and woman were holding hands. We were happy and joyful. Death came again. The same scene again. The same bed, the same room, the same people. And her. The missing piece was complete. My wife was there too, holding my hand. I felt her love for me. My life was complete.

'I don't know to this day if that person was me or from another life. I do know that something inside me shifted with the alternative ending to that story. I also feel like I experienced death, what death feels like, through the death of that man. The freeing of energy, or spirit, away from the body. I also know this. I went to Sabari with two litres of fluid in my right lung. She said with complete certainty that the fluid would go by the time we finished our work. That is exactly what happened.

'A couple of months later, while continuing with my medicines, I had completely recovered from the illness.

I had been going through the same medical treatment earlier, but the fluid kept coming back. However, after my healing sessions, my body responded to the medical treatment as well, and I was healed. I can now vouch for the fact that hidden emotions can physically affect our bodies.'

Colours of the rainbow

Healing works differently for different people. For me, it is important to understand the uniqueness of the person I am working with and respect that. A single key cannot unlock all locks. Some are sceptics initially, some have checked out many modes of therapy before landing up at my clinic, some have a negative orientation towards life, some come with denial, some are trying to run away from issues by being overtly religious and 'spiritual', some are intensely controlling and do not know surrender, some are so depressed and tired that they have no life-force energy, some are victims of abuse and malpractice ... Well, the list can go on. The healer/therapist needs to hold space for all kinds of clients and give them a feeling of security so they can heal themselves. I create that space for their healing, give them tools and know-how to shed excess emotional baggage and be free.

Healing always has to come from within for real, long-term transformation to happen. It is a soul choice for every client who visits a healer, a therapist, because you cannot rejuvenate anyone if they choose not to let go. It is important always to remember the adage: 'You can lead a horse to water, but you can't make him drink.'

The Chinese believe in yin and yang, two opposite forces that govern everything in this world. The yin–yang philosophy says that the universe is composed of competing and complementary forces of dark and light, sun and moon, male and female. This thought is more than 3,500 years old and deeply influences the philosophies of Taoism and Confucianism.

Actually, this duality of universal energies is found in most religions and philosophical belief systems around the world. Christians believe in heaven and hell, salvation and suffering, God and Satan, etc. Hindu philosophy talks about dharma and adharma, good and bad, duality and non-duality, saint and sinner, etc.

Jews, Buddhists, Muslims and every other sect have the same concepts of light and darkness, passive and active, male and female, faith and non-faith and so on.

We all have darkness and light in our mental/emotional landscapes as well. We live by balancing these two forces, but when either goes out of balance, things become unmanageable for us, and we must start looking for help. Too much light can be overwhelming—imagine your third eye has opened up and you start seeing the aura or the energy fields of everyone who is passing you by, or you become so involved in spiritual practices that you remove yourself from family duties and forget to pay your child's school tuition fees.

Even the most elevated soul has to find synergy between the inner and outer self when in a family setting, fulfilling the duties of grihastha (the householder) in life's journey. The ancient sages of India beautifully divided life into four stages of existence. In Hinduism, they are called 'ashramas', and individuals were encouraged to follow them for a harmonious life. They are, in order:

1. Brahmacharya, or the student stage
2. Grihastha, or the householder stage
3. Vanaprastha, or the hermit stage
4. Sannyasa, or the wandering ascetic stage

The third and fourth ashramas are more or less obsolete in this frenetic, modern world most of us live in. At fifty to sixty years of age, the phase in which the sages suggested gradual withdrawal from the life of the householder (to the vanaprastha stage), we are super active at work in senior positions, heading businesses and organizations, and involved heavily in the household with getting children married or becoming engaged grandfathers and grandmothers. There is nothing wrong with that. But through the vagaries of life and the weight of its expectations, knowingly or unknowingly, we might forget to practise that which brings light and healing into our lives.

Some people, I have seen, have the wisdom and inner knowledge to self-heal. They are divinely guided; their subconscious minds know how to heal themselves and fill their beings with light. Such people might be externally doing their duties in the physical world, but internally their minds might be silently practising the various ashramas.

Many may not be so lucky. They might need a conduit who can help them get in touch with their own powers and channel that power into their minds and bodies to live in harmony.

In this regard, a powerful mantra to chant is 'Aham aarogyam', which translates to 'I am healthy'. The affirmation to the body that it is healthy and disease-free can feel wonderful, energetically, to both the body and mind.

In the Bible (Matthew 7:7, New Testament), it says: 'Ask, and it shall be given you; seek, and ye shall find; knock, and it shall be opened unto you. For every one that asketh receiveth; and he that seeketh findeth; and to him that knocketh it shall be opened.'

I have always, unequivocally, embraced the deeper essence of the verse above. In every field of life, I believe, you just need to ask with deep intent in your heart to receive—be it healing, abundance or love. When one has the courage to embrace healing, healing shows up and the shackles are unshackled.

Here is the story of an exceptionally talented lady, in her own words. She came to see me in 2012, when she could not handle her mental and emotional situation any longer.

'I have been married for several years and have two amazing preteen children. I met this man, whom I had heard was super rich, influential and a total Casanova. The first time I met him was at a party, and I avoided him completely. Later that night, when I was leaving, he came up to me and gave me his business card. But I refused to take the card.

'However, we kept bumping into each other at common friends' get-togethers, and we ended up becoming friends. He started calling me every day and we would chat for hours. I didn't realize when, during those phone calls, I began to develop feelings for him. Not that we ever had anything physical, but I was falling in love with him in a pure, special way.

'One fine day, he accused me of something I never did and stopped talking to me. I could not handle this rejection. I tried to explain that I had not done anything wrong. He knew my state of mind and started playing mind games with me. I was completely broken and hurt and was willing to do anything to fix this relationship, even though nothing was my fault. The more I tried to mend this rift, the more pleasure it gave him to mentally torture me. I was completely broken inside, and it was beyond me to get a hold of myself. I would cry bitterly, feeling helpless, and obviously could not share anything with anyone at home. Bodily, I felt suffocated, my heart broken and terribly depressed. I was inches away from a total nervous breakdown. *I needed help!*

'I got to know about this therapist, and I was told by a friend that she would be able to help me. It took some courage on my part to fix the appointment. The day finally arrived when I actually met her—totally broken, anxious, fidgety, nervous and in emotional agony. Sabari Chakraborty asked me to tell her my story, but I just didn't know where to start. She encouraged me to talk so that we could be on the same page. But it was so difficult for me to start, as the moment I tried to speak, I would burst out crying uncontrollably.

'Sabari did not ask me to stop crying or go on crying; she just quietly placed a box of tissues in front of me. I would dab my eyes, try to start and then burst out crying again ... This just went on. There were moments when she would just silently look at me, and all I felt was: "How scary is this lady!" In my mind, I was a poor victim, suffering, and this therapist did not understand.

'Eventually, I grew so comfortable with Sabari that I signed up for many more sessions. I started pouring my heart out. My mother died when I was three years old, and a lot of hidden anxieties and childhood traumas surfaced when I was made to feel like a victim. With absolute patience and gentle handholding, she helped me realize how all my hidden fears came from my own internal space. Taking baby steps through therapy, I was able to clear and resolve so many hidden emotions. Today I am an empowered human being, even though life has thrown many challenges in my direction. I am no longer helpless, and I can overcome my challenges.

'I am so glad I made that phone call to Sabari so many years ago, met her and addressed my issues. I will always hold great love and respect for Sabari all my life.'

—*Anu Rungta (name changed on request), forty-five years old, chef*

When to see a healer

1. When there is a feeling of sadness or anxiety within you that is seeping into all facets of your life.

2. When there is a sense of depression and negative feelings without any known plausible triggers. This includes long-term depression and short bouts as well.
3. When emotions are hampering your normal day-to-day functioning—such as extreme anger, jealousy, grief, fear of survival, need for constant love and admiration, etc.
4. When patterns are repeating themselves in your life. For example, if every relationship you enter inevitably ends, if you are fired from all your jobs without any fault of your own, if you are falling ill repeatedly out of the blue, etc.
5. When you are battling any kind of addiction—alcohol, drugs, sex, food or gambling, to name a few.
6. Last but not least, when you want to connect with the deepest part of your being and know yourself better. A guide/healer/therapist can work effectively with your subconscious and enhance your journey of looking within.

Look out for red flags

Many a time, a person needing help is either in denial of their issues or scared to seek help for various reasons. It could be a fear of being judged by society or thinking that internal issues can be dealt with by oneself.

Here comes the vital role that family, friends and well-wishers can play. A lot of times we tend not to interfere in the 'private affairs' of other people and may look the other way even if we notice certain anomalies. However, in mental-emotional imbalances, when the affected person does not have the will or desire to seek help, a firm nudge or creating awareness to encourage them to meet a professional therapist or healer is always the right thing to do. These are important conversations, albeit delicate, and may go the extra mile to save a life.

> *'Healing doesn't mean the damage never existed. It means the damage no longer controls our lives.'*
> **—Akshay Dubey, CEO, CVW CleanTech**

Chapter 3
How to Cleanse Your Aura

'"Aura" is what one reflects in the heart, what you bring into the world and what people want to learn from you.'

—Ozuna

In common parlance, we use the word 'aura' quite loosely and frequently—how a particular person has a certain calmness in their aura, or has an attractive, warm aura, or a negative aura and so on. We tend to use the word 'aura' to describe a certain energy or vibration that we receive from a person, or even a place.

The aura is the electromagnetic field around animate and inanimate objects or their subtle bodies, which makes up their energy signatures. This energy field also emanates colours and light based on the frequency of its vibration.

In 1939, an interesting phenomenon was observed by a Russian electrical engineer named Semyon Kirlian and his wife, Valentina, whose experiments with this phenomenon led to the development of a photographic process now known as Kirlian photography.

'[They] developed Kirlian photography after observing a patient in Krasnodar Hospital who was receiving medical treatment from a high-frequency electrical generator. They had noticed that when the electrodes were brought near the patient's skin, there was a glow similar to that of a neon discharge tube.

'The Kirlians conducted experiments in which photographic film was placed on top of a conducting plate, and another conductor was attached to a hand, a leaf or other plant material. The conductors were energized by a high-frequency high-voltage power source, producing photographic images typically showing a silhouette of the object surrounded by an aura of light.

'In 1958, the Kirlians reported the results of their experiments for the first time. Their work was virtually unknown until 1970, when two Americans, Lynn Schroeder and Sheila Ostrander, published a book, *Psychic Discoveries Behind the Iron Curtain*. High-voltage electrophotography soon became known to the general public as Kirlian photography.'[1]

---

[1] 'Kirlian photography', Wikipedia, https://en.wikipedia.org/wiki/Kirlian_photography.

I had read about Kirlian photography, and in the mid-1990s, I had an opportunity to actually see the Kirlian photography process in Khareghat Colony in Mumbai. Agog with curiosity, I sat in a hall where the demonstration was to be held. I was pleasantly surprised to see a few Mumbai celebrities, along with Riz Khan, a CNN newsreader and political commentator whom I liked very much, present as well.

After an introductory talk, the demonstration began with a head of broccoli. The camera showed the aura around the broccoli, which was a vivid, bright purple.

Next, we were shown the aura around a human being. A volunteer from the audience walked up to the stage. We were all waiting with bated breath to see the energy field around the volunteer's physical body. Lo and behold! The Kirlian camera showed the volunteer's aura to every person present in that hall. His aura was red and yellow, the colours merging into each other. At that time, seeing this felt quite spectacular. Later, aura readers would take photographs on a white background and scan the picture with an aura-reading scanner, and the printout would show the etheric body in different colours.

Some people are clairsentient and can read auras with the naked eye. I am blessed—I happen to be one of them. I can read an aura through a photograph as well and sense people's energies even if they are not physically in front of me. This 'detection' ability feels fortunate at times, as it helps in my healing work immensely, but at other times, it feels unfortunate, such as when I walk into a social gathering, say hello to strangers and immediately have my clairsentient radar detect their energy signatures, or their auras. Over the years, I have learnt to subdue this radar when it is too strong for the occasion.

The different types of auric bodies

The physical body is the body we can touch, feel and see. Made up of bones, muscles, tissues, etc., this is the densest body and requires air, food, water, exercise and rest. However, besides the tangible physical body, we also have seven subtle energy bodies that make up our aura. They are:

1. **The etheric body:** This is the first invisible body, closest to the physical body, and the subtle body that some therapists/healers/shamans can see with the naked eye. It is approximately two to four inches away from the physical body, and energy healers work with this body many a time to identify the cause of and to heal dis-eases.

2. **The emotional body:** This is outside of the etheric body, extending one to three inches. This layer is connected to the sacral chakra and holds all our strong emotions, feelings and perceptions, like happiness, sadness, love, hate, etc.

3. **The mental body:** This comes after the emotional body and is connected to the solar plexus chakra, containing all our mental thought processes, such as rules, judgements and ethics.

4. The astral body: This is the bridge between the lower vibrations of the physical plane and the higher vibrations of the spiritual. Connected to the heart chakra, it is a very important subtle body, like a treasure house of our spiritual experiences, and is less dense than the four bodies mentioned above. When we have out-of-body experiences, this is the body to which we are connected.

5. **The celestial body:** This is the body that connects us to the divine. Through the heart chakra, the celestial body allows us to reach a level of awareness and connectedness that aligns us with the universe. The celestial body vibrates on the frequency of pure bliss and unconditional love. The celestial body is activated during deep meditative states.

6. **The causal body:** This is sometimes referred to as the soul because it holds all of the information of the lower bodies, as well as the consciousness of our oneness with the divine. This has a very high vibrational frequency, and people

connected with their causal body intrinsically know that they are one with the universe. The causal body is also thought to be the part of you that reincarnates. After each life, the causal body retains the information of the other bodies below it and takes that into the next life. When people connect to their past lives through hypnosis, it is often through the causal body.

7. **The spiritual body:** This seventh body can extend up to three feet or more. Connected to the crown chakra, it vibrates to the highest frequency of positive energy. When the physical body makes a connection with the spiritual body, it operates from its highest consciousness.

No two auras are identical, and auras are constantly shifting because of changes in our thought/emotional/spiritual patterns. When we are low on energy and feeling negative emotions, our aura naturally shrinks to reflect this. And when we are happy, our aura expands, radiating outwards. This phenomenon explains why we are innately attracted to happier people and less attracted to negative people. Well, unless, of course, we are also in a negative mindset—then we are naturally attracted to other negative people. One of the laws of the universe is that the people we attract are connected to the vibrational frequency of our electromagnetic field, both negative and positive.

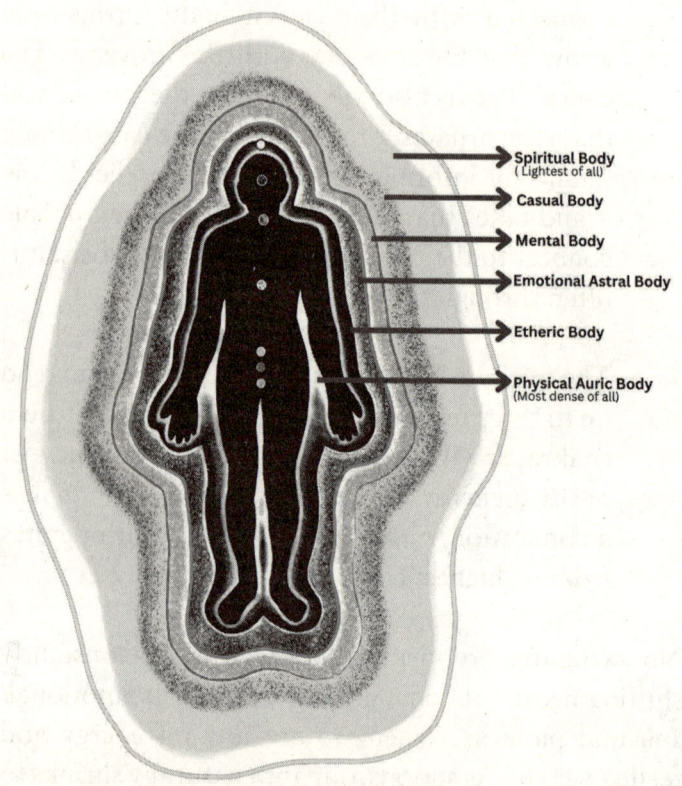

Many names for the same energy

Modern science has not been able to directly measure these subtle bodies, but scientists have studied enough of their effects to confirm their existence.[2]

---

[2] JJ Loizzo, 'The subtle body: an interoceptive map of central nervous system function and meditative mind-brain-body integration', (Ann N Y Acad Sci. June 2016) p. 78–95.

It is also an ongoing area of research in the field of quantum physics. Alternative medicine and ancient traditions have used subtle energy in their spiritual practices and healing rituals for centuries. Across cultures, subtle energy goes by many different names: prana in Sanskrit, qi in Chinese, mana in Polynesian and ki in Japanese.[3]

Subtle energy is life-force energy, and different cultures have worked with it in different ways. Reiki, pranic healing, shamanism, tai chi, alternative medicine and energy healing positively harness this energy to harmonize our auric bodies for health and our emotional and spiritual well-being.

In our earthly lives, we deal with traumas, big and small, on a moment-to-moment basis. This can make us feel tired and anxious, and surround our auras in a pall of heavy grey energy (or a shadowy pall of gloom).

In my sessions, as the client sits down and starts talking, invariably their aura starts becoming more and more visible to me. This is especially evident with the ones who are unwell or depressed or fearful—their auras are so heavy that they are visible right away. It has taken me years of practice, meditation and objectivity not to get overwhelmed or affected by acutely negative

---

[3] JJ Loizzo, 'The subtle body: an interoceptive map of central nervous system function and meditative mind-brain-body integration', (Ann N Y Acad Sci. June 2016), p. 78–95.

auras and to direct my energy towards the client's aura cleansing and healing needs.

How our auras get disrupted

Some clients call me up specifically for aura cleansings when they are not 'feeling themselves' and suspect something has gone awry in their energy space. Some have picked up negative energies in their electromagnetic fields but are not consciously aware that they have and continue to feel burdened and low.

Negative emotions and energies can enter our aura when the aura is 'open'. These emotions and energies are not necessarily ours but are picked up in our energy fields when we are vulnerable—in the grip of strong emotions (like anger, grief and fear)—or when our physical and metaphysical energy is weak because of illness or substance abuse.

Our energy bodies can open up and render our physical bodies vulnerable, especially in the case of sudden head injuries. At the top of the head is the crown chakra. The crown chakra, or Sahasrāra (a thousand-petalled lotus) chakra in Sanskrit, is known as 'the bridge to the cosmos'. Located above the crown of the head, it is our centre of higher knowledge and wisdom and is our connection to divine guidance. A head injury can fracture the harmony of our energy field, leading to physical symptoms like blurry vision, headaches, migraines and even blackouts.

Our auras can also open up due to substance abuse, like drugs and alcohol. When inebriated, balance gives way to dis-balance, leaving our energy bodies open, wounded and vulnerable.

As mentioned above, very strong negative emotions and violent behaviours can also create absolute disharmony in our electromagnetic fields. Nobody likes to be around an angry, depressed or violent person, as their aura can feel too heavy for people who are not in that negative zone, and it can also drain their energy.

Anaesthesia opens up our aura as well. Induced anaesthesia for surgeries, even dental surgeries, opens up the aura. When the energy system of the body goes into unconsciousness or a particular area is numbed through medical intervention, such as an opioid or anaesthetic gas, all the bodies go into disarray and the aura opens up. Later in the chapter, I will share tips on how you can seal and protect your aura, even if you have to undergo anaesthesia for surgery.

Very loud, thumping music frazzles our energy bodies, causing the aura to open up. Psychotropic medication, taken over a period of time, can open the aura. Hence, it is imperative and prudent to take the advice of your doctor if you wish to discontinue any psychotropic medication because the medicine needs to be brought down to smaller doses before it is stopped. It is not good to suddenly stop any psychotropic medication as this can have adverse effects.

External entities

When our energy bodies are in disarray, we are open to getting entities stuck in our auric fields.

An 'entity' is a soul like you or me but without a physical body. Souls, though disembodied, have not been able to go through what the Tibetans call 'the Bardo', or the gateway to the 'other side'. So these entities are stuck on earth and near-earth realms, sometimes accidentally and sometimes not so accidentally. In popular media, they are the heroes and heroines of 'ghost' movies.

I don't like to call them ghosts but spirits who are stuck in this dimension. Some of these entities might not even know that they are not entirely in their physical bodies and are dead in that sense. Spirit is energy. We are all energy, but that energy is held in a receptacle called 'the body', or else energy would combust in this atomically packed plane we call earth. Combustion will happen when exposed without a vehicle for an extended period of time.

These entities/energies automatically look for a receptacle or body when they don't have a physical body to stay in on this plane. When our auras are open, entities can enter our energetic space and stay there for many earth years without one even consciously making a connection. Symptoms might be felt in the form of:

- mood alterations
- changes in energy levels

- feeling an invisible presence
- nightmares or, in some cases, suicidal thoughts or depression
- unexplained aches and pains.

In many cases, I found that these entities stay behind because they have a specific job to finish or a specific message to pass on. And some entities, as mentioned, do not know when the spirit-body connection was severed, especially in cases of sudden accidental deaths. These confused entities take refuge in the first open aura they find—their floating energy finds a receptacle.

The entities who choose not to cross over to the spirit world, our real home, do so because of emotional reasons. Themes of revenge, caring, love, violence, fear, etc., get played out here. Like a mother who does not want to leave her beloved son alone in the earth realm even though she is physically dead, or a loving husband trying to protect his vulnerable wife by being around her, possibly in her aura space, making her sense his presence constantly and sometimes feel reassured but sometimes fall deeper into her grief, there are many emotion-driven reasons that entities stay behind.

Sometimes an entity may choose to stay back on the earth plane because of addiction. A soul who was addicted to drugs or alcohol and wants to continue feeling the high finds the open aura of a human addict and enters their energy space to feed off the person's addiction. If you like to hang out in bars and nightclubs or where people are doing drugs, or even in your own home, pay attention to the section where I talk about how to seal your aura.

Here is an interesting story of an Indian Army jawan (a foot soldier) who found me online and came to me for an aura cleansing. He was a well-built man but looked tired and pale when he came to see me. He walked into my clinic and said without any hesitation that he needed an aura cleansing. Curious, I asked: 'How are you so sure you need an aura cleansing?'

'Because I feel tired constantly, my energy levels are at zero and I feel a heaviness in my body. I don't feel like myself,' he answered.

After gathering a little more information about his life in the army and his current emotional state, we got to work.

After the induction, he entered a state of meditative trance, and in the aura cleansing session, it was revealed that there was indeed an entity in his space. It was the soul of a road accident victim who was still grappling with the severance between the soul and the physical body.

My client, the jawan, while on a bus to Nagpur to see his family, had stopped at a dhaba to eat some dinner and had ventured out for a short walk to stretch his legs. For some reason, the jawan's aura was open, and the disoriented entity, looking for a receptacle to hold its disembodied energy, entered the jawan's auric space.

This might sound extreme and unbelievable to certain readers, but I have personally experienced this in hundreds of entity clearings that I have facilitated.

Aura cleansing and sealing done, the jawan said he was feeling a bit woozy but definitely lighter. I could see that his skin was looking clearer and his eyes brighter and more focused.

Two days later, he called me excitedly, saying he felt like his old, energetic self again and that he was very happy. I reminded him to continue to seal his aura, as I had taught him to do.

Dark magic

However unpleasant it is, I need to bring to your notice another kind of entity takeover of the human aura that is a premeditated and directed invasion with malintent of our energy space. Since it is real, we cannot sidestep the topic of black magic.

Most of us have heard or read about black magic at least once in our lives. We might also have heard about white magic for that matter. White magic is the domain of spells and natural remedies to find love, keep optimal health, attract abundance or find a good job.

Wicca is considered to be white magic. 'Wicca is a modern-day, nature-based pagan religion. Though rituals and practices vary among people who identify as Wiccan, most observations include the festival celebrations of solstices and equinoxes, the honoring of a male god and a female goddess, and the incorporation of herbalism and other natural objects into rituals. Wiccans practice their religion according to an ethical code, and many believe in reincarnation.'[4]

There are genuine practitioners of Wicca all over the world who practise this pagan occultism and aim to do more good than harm.

However, black magic is practised only to do harm, to inflict damage.

While growing up in Kolkata, I heard stories about evil being intentionally inflicted upon families and human beings. I never believed those stories and never cared about black magic. But as I started delving deeper into occult and spiritual practices, travelled around and met more like-minded people, I was forced to sit up and take notice of this thing called 'black magic'.

While I was working in an advertising firm, one day, a colleague shared with me the story of his father's death. My colleague's father, who had lived in south India, was a perfectly healthy man who loved pottering around in his garden. Out of the blue, he had a massive heart attack and passed away immediately. The devastated family conducted his last rites, shocked at how a healthy man had died so suddenly. A month after the tragedy, a holy man visited their house and asked my colleague's mother if there was a mango tree

---

[4] https://www.history.com/topics/religion/wicca.

in the garden. She confirmed that there was one. The holy man asked her to dig around the roots of that tree.

Curious, my colleague's mother asked someone to dig around the tree, and she found a copper plate on which there were some indentations resembling a mantra. They were indecipherable to her. She asked the holy man what this thing was, and the holy man said that black magic had been performed on her husband, causing a healthy man to die suddenly. Apparently, the holy man had sensed this through his clairvoyance and, hence, had asked her to dig around the roots of that particular tree. He had also said that the black magic had been performed by the dead man's sister, as she wanted the entire ancestral property. My colleague clarified that his father and his aunt had indeed shared a very bad relationship and had been bickering over the ancestral property for decades. But the holy man had not known this when he named the perpetrator.

I was gobsmacked! I would have swatted this story away but for the fact that this well-educated, modern young man himself did not understand the concept of black magic and was simply narrating to me the series of events as they had unfolded.

It gave me food for thought, and what I had earlier swept aside as 'nonsense' slowly started making sense when I began talking to different people about it. Black magic is practised all over India, Southeast Asia and among aboriginal tribes worldwide, and it is quite rampant. Little did I know that in a few years, I would be cleansing people's auras from hostile takeovers by spirits who have been programmed to harm people.

I am yet to see how practitioners of black magic programme a lost soul, one without a physical body, and redirect its energies into someone's energy field. However, the intended person's aura must be energetically open for the programmed soul to enter their body. If your energy bodies are in harmony and well-sealed, the malefic intent of black magic practitioners does not succeed.

Funnily, sometimes entities are invited by YOU! Yes, it's true. Oftentimes, when we are in distress or pain, we call out loudly, 'Someone, please help me!' Entities floating around, especially those familiar with the kind of distress you are going through, respond to your call and enter your space to 'help you'. They start managing areas of your life in which you feel challenged. These entities are like rent-free tenants in your electromagnetic field, and they obviously need not be there. A few people I know also use entities to manage their business or their money, and they willingly hand over the programming of their lives to these 'helpful' beings. As astonishingly bizarre as it sounds, it's true.

When people come to me for aura cleansings, I use some simple cleansing tools to release the entity, help it cross over into the light and seal the client's aura. Some entities reside in the physical body, causing aches, pains and dis-eases, and some are stuck to the aura. If the aura is open, entities who vibrate at your frequency will naturally be drawn to you. Angry entities get drawn to angry people, depressed entities are attracted to depressed people, souls who have passed over due to substance abuse like to attach themselves to the aura of addicts on the earth plane, and so on and so forth. The existing condition of depression or addiction goes notches higher when a like-minded energy is residing in your space.

I also clear entities who have been sent to harm someone through black magic. These entities are usually damaged through some bad experience on earth and are easy to manipulate. They are programmed and weaponized with malevolent intent to cause harm, so they initially refuse to go into the divine light and back home into the spirit world. But once they see or feel the divine presence surrounding them, with some guidance and fear removal, they surrender into the light. They are free and the client is free from the evil machinations of practitioners of black magic. Since karma spares no one, these practitioners also pay the price for harming people intentionally. All I can say is stay away from black magic, however tempting it might seem as a tool to control another person's life.

Aura cleansings are usually done in one session, but if the programming is too strong and the client's life-force energy a bit weak, it can extend to two sessions max, but not more than that.

How to cleanse and seal your aura

The cleansing tips given below can be done by you easily on a daily, weekly or monthly basis. When you are feeling heavy or bogged down physically, mentally or emotionally, it is a good time to cleanse and seal your aura. However, if it is a black magic possession or a severe case of disturbance in your electromagnetic field, I advise you to go to a trained therapist or someone who is an expert in aura cleansing.

Crystal clearing

Crystals are stones or solids with highly diverse molecules and atoms, forming a unique design that shows through. They are known to absorb negative energies naturally. A pure crystal that keeps 'energy vampires' from feeding on your energies and also clears negative energies fabulously is an amethyst crystal, which comes in shades of purple.

A black obsidian crystal also keeps away negative energies and gives protection.

A clear quartz crystal is a master healer crystal, but it also amplifies everything—both good and bad. So a clear quartz should be charged with positive intentions before placing it anywhere. It is connected to the seventh chakra above the crown of your head and is great for a meditation room, etc. For a harmonious romantic relationship with a partner, keep a pink quartz in your bedroom, preferably on the bedside table.

Be aware of the source of the crystal so that you are not duped into buying a fake. Do a little research and find a genuine dealer in crystals, as crystals are sourced from all over the world. Ask for a certification of purity or the mine or country it has been sourced from. Always buy from a trusted person.

Crystals need to be energized both before and after use. To energize the crystal, wash it thoroughly in salt water, pat it dry and keep it for around three days to soak in moonlight during the period of the waxing moon going towards the full moon. Then just before use, place the crystal on your left palm, cover it with your right palm and, from your heart, say to the crystal, 'I welcome your positive, healing energies into my life to help me cleanse all unwanted negative energies that do not belong to me.'

Your crystal is now ready for use.

Hold the crystal (a longish pencil-like shape is best for aura cleansing), and from the top of your head to your feet, move the crystal lengthwise to cleanse the auric space around you. Move the crystal around your whole body, top to bottom and sideways, but not too fast. This ritual takes just a few minutes but needs to be done with intent and attention.

After you have done the crystal cleansing thoroughly, put the crystal in a fresh bowl of salt water, clean it, place it in moonlight to charge for three days and put it away on your altar or any place that is sacred to you. Do the cleansing for 5–7 minutes or till you feel satisfied.

Saltwater baths and sealing the aura with high-vibrational white light

For centuries, it has been believed that salt crystals can naturally absorb negative energy. When the aura feels out of kilter, soak some rock salt crystals in a bucket or bowl of water and have a saltwater bath. You can also put rock salt in a bathtub if you have one, and soak in it. While having a saltwater bath, focus on the positive intention of cleansing your body of any negative vibrations or energies.

Post the bath (do not wash off the salt crystals with water; let them stay on your skin for a while), visualize yourself being surrounded by a bright, clean white light. Imagine a bubble all around you, from your head to your feet. Soak in the light and imagine you are zipping the light all around you, so your physical and other energy bodies are in a protective bubble of light.

Cleansing the aura with white sage or camphor

This process is called 'smudging' and is quite effective in protecting the aura. Smudging is quite an ancient practice in which a bunch of dried sage is lit and moved lengthwise from the head to the toes, allowing the smoke to circulate around your body. Keep a plate or clam-shell bowl in your left hand so the ashes don't drop on you or on the floor.

Some camphor pellets can be lit in a small brass bowl with a handle, and it can be moved around the body in the same way as during a sage smudging. This can be done once a month or more frequently, when ever one is feeling an energy imbalance. Do this cleansing in the daylight hours.

Using sounds and fragrances for cleansing
Ringing bells, playing singing bowls, listening to the tinkling of wind chimes, lighting fragrant incense sticks with the aroma of sandalwood, lavender or jasmine and allowing the sounds and fragrances to waft around us and in our space aligns our chakras and helps keep positive energy circulating in our electromagnetic field, making us feel balanced and harmonious.

When our five senses are attuned to nature's sounds, aromas and rhythms, our mind and body feel calm and tranquil. Take a deep dive into the changing seasons; observe how nature adapts and blooms through the changing weather, through the heat, cold and rain, and yet holds space for us to recuperate in her arms.

So go on—allow the self-healing to start and deepen your self-love with these simple remedies.

Chapter 4

Inner Child Therapy: Healing Childhood Traumas That Get Carried into Adulthood

'Hold the hand of the child that lives in your soul. For this child, nothing is impossible.'
—Paulo Coelho

In the ancient Shiva Mahapurana, a profound tale of a father and son unfolds, revealing a journey of trauma followed by healing. This captivating narrative, found amidst the vast tapestry of Hindu mythology, sheds light on the enigmatic nature of Shiva, the Supreme God and the creator of the universe alongside Brahma and Vishnu. Known as 'the destroyer', Shiva is the bestower of blessings and curses, holding within himself the essence of all healing.

Let us delve into this enthralling story, drawn from the popular version found in the Shiva Purana. It begins with Shiva's frequent travels, leaving behind his beloved consort, Parvati, who would often find herself consumed by loneliness in his absence. In her yearning for his presence, Parvati unknowingly neglected her own well-being, forgetting to tend to her personal hygiene, lost in the depths of her longing. In her desperate state, she conceived an idea to create a child for herself.

Laxmi and Saraswati, her two grown-up daughters, were preoccupied with their own responsibilities and households, leaving Parvati with a longing to nurture a child of her own. With great determination, she shaped a figure out of the accumulated dirt on her body and breathed life into it. Thus, Ganesha, her handsome newborn son, came into being.[1] Parvati's heart was filled with joy, and she found solace in the presence of her beloved child.

The dynamics between Shiva and Ganesha, father and son, are quite intricate and interesting.

We are well aware of the immense power and wrath that Shiva possesses as 'the destroyer of the world'. However, in this tale, Shiva's actions take an unexpected turn, as he finds himself committing an extreme act of violence. The legend in the Shiva Purana recounts that Shiva was away on an expedition, unaware of the existence of his newborn son, Ganesha.

---

[1] https://forum.philosophynow.org/viewtopic.php?t=39092.

In Shiva's absence, Parvati entrusted Ganesha with the task of guarding the entrance while she indulged in her bathing rituals. It was at this precise moment that Shiva, oblivious to Ganesha's relation to him, returned home. Despite the hermits and devas attempting to persuade him, the dutiful Ganesha refused to grant Shiva entry into his mother's sanctum. His unwavering loyalty rested solely with his mother, causing his father's wrath to ignite.

What ensued was a tumultuous clash between father and son, akin to a fierce battle. Tragically, this confrontation culminated in Shiva beheading his own son. Parvati, stricken with grief, pleaded with her husband to breathe life back into their son's headless body. Touched by her profound sorrow and love, Shiva granted her plea, replacing Ganesha's severed head with that of an elephant. In an extraordinary twist of fate, the elephant god, Gajanana (the one with an elephant's head), was reborn.

While it is natural for ideological differences and disagreements to arise between parents and children, the savage act that unfolded in the realm of the gods should undoubtedly be condemned. In the matrix, there existed numerous alternative ways to address Ganesha's behaviour, and resorting to such extreme measures driven by rage was indeed an excessive response. But 'tatha bhavatu,' or so be it.

Through this poignant tale, we are reminded of the complexities that reside within the realm of gods and goddesses. It reveals the multifaceted nature of Shiva, who, despite being 'the destroyer', can also be moved by compassion and love. It teaches us that healing and renewal can arise even from the darkest depths of tragedy, transforming a father's regrettable act into an opportunity for redemption and the birth of a divine deity—the revered elephant god, Ganesha.

In the vast expanse of Hindu mythology, stories such as these serve as mirrors, reflecting the intricacies of human emotions and relationships. They offer insights into the eternal dance of creation and destruction, of sorrow and healing, unveiling the timeless wisdom hidden within the folds of ancient texts.

In the manushya loka, or the human world, inner children are created when the child feels unloved, judged or abandoned by their caregivers.

In the heart of a child resides the emotional empowerment of the adult.

Who is the 'inner child'?

Many trace the concept of an inner child to Carl Jung, a Swiss psychiatrist and psychoanalyst practising in the early 1900s, who described a child archetype in his work. In *The Psychology of the Child Archetype*, Volume 9, Jung wrote:

> 'The "eternal child" in man is an indescribable experience, an incongruity, a handicap, and a divine prerogative; an imponderable that

determines the ultimate worth or worthlessness of a personality.'

This is the 'divine child' archetype.

Along with lightness and playfulness, a child in adverse situations has also felt sad, abandoned, frustrated and anxious at various junctures while growing up. Early experiences play a very important part in our development as an adult. When the experiences are positive, there are higher chances that the adult will be a balanced personality. However, if the experiences have been scarring, frightening or abusive, they can negatively affect the adult personality. Hence, all these sub-parts require healing and assimilation, so these wounds do not get carried into adulthood and our decision-making powers are not overwhelmed by painful triggers from our childhood.

The two universal truths

There are two universal truths that do not change for any of us. The first is that each of us has a belief system from which we operate. This belief system starts forming when we are in the mother's womb, before birth, and solidifies by the time we are fifteen or sixteen years old, with puberty being the time for difficult transformations.

From my own sessions and general research as well, it has been established that the soul in the womb can sense the feelings of the parents, especially the mother, and other external circumstances.[2]

Even in the foetal state, impressions are being created and held on to. Then, of course, the learnings from childhood and puberty. Once we finish with our teen years, through our education, our experiences through travel and interactions with people, we create a personality that we would like to exhibit to the world, wanting the world to perceive us a certain way—as a funny person, a studious person, a caring person, an adventurous person, and so on and so forth.

However, whenever a crisis or an emotionally critical situation arises in adulthood, the behaviour we will display in handling that critical situation largely comes from the belief system that we learnt in our early years of existence, which has taken root and solidified by the time we are sixteen years old. If there are unhealed inner children who have felt abandoned or experienced other negative emotions, they will rear their heads from the womb of the unconscious and display aberrant behaviour whenever there is a challenging situation in adulthood.

The second universal truth is that a female child subliminally, subconsciously learns from the primary female caregiver, which is the mother. If the

---

[2] M Araki, S Nishitani, K Ushimaru, H Masuzaki, K Oishi, K Shinohara, 'Fetal response to induced maternal emotions.' J Physiol Sci., May 2010; https://www.pmc.ncbi.nlm.nih.gov/articles/PMC10717758/.

mother is dead or not available, the girl child will then learn from the secondary female caregiver—a grandmother, older sister, aunt, etc. This learning is not particularly a conscious bid to learn, but it is more of a subconscious process of learning by observing the adult.

In the same fashion, a male child learns directly from the primary male caregiver, which is the father. If the father is not around, he will learn from other male role models, like the grandfather, elder brother, uncle, etc. This too is a subliminal, subconscious process of learning.

Inner children are created through traumatic incidents and also through the learnt behaviour that we imbibe from our primary or secondary caregivers.

Why is integrating and healing the inner child so important to be a well-functioning adult?

It is because it gives us the capability to deal with crises in our lives with wisdom and maturity.

For example, if a forty-year-old adult woman has serious arguments with her adult partner or husband in which she feels abandoned and unloved, it can be an indication of an unhealed inner child. Adults can resolve conflicts with conversations, even some number of compromises, but when an argument spirals someone into feelings of abandonment, it shows that this emotional trigger might be coming from an unhealed and deep trauma, when the adult might have felt unloved and abandoned in their childhood. The triggers remained because that emotional void was never filled or addressed.

And as for learnt behaviour from caregivers, triggers are hidden there as well, regarding how we will be as adults.

The penny drops

Many years ago, around 2015, a woman in her thirties came to see me for some career issues. She was bright and intelligent, but her professional life always felt like an uphill struggle, and she was not as successful as she should have been. In the first session, as we were talking, I mentioned the two universal truths to her. She screwed up her nose and said, 'No, that is not true. I dislike my mother intensely for her uncontrollable anger and the way she shouts and screams. I am not like her at all. I never display such crass behaviour.' I did not contradict her.

After the next session, which was about trying to figure out why her professional life was not going the way she wanted it to go, my client said, 'Oh my god!' She was goggle-eyed with some deep revelation. I wanted her to join the dots for herself, so I asked, 'What happened?'

She said, 'I am exactly like my mother! I have deep-seated anger, but I never express it by screaming or shouting. I try to keep a calm exterior even when I am seething inside. I clearly have issues with authority figures and have never been able to get along with my bosses, so my career suffered. I always blamed my bosses because I never showed them my displeasure or anger overtly, but surely they must have picked it up. I was self-sabotaging my career with my hidden anger!'

As my client identified correctly, negative learned behaviour will create a pattern of self-sabotage, no matter how calm we try to appear from the outside. It does not harm anyone but us, as we start feeling not good enough, curb our growth subconsciously and unknowingly stymie our own progress. Obviously her bosses were picking up the vibrations of her animosity, knowingly or unknowingly, and she was not creating a favourable impression in her bosses' minds. Hence, my client was not fully supported in her office atmosphere, and her career was suffering because of her passive-aggressive behaviour.

Since earth is a tough school in which we learn deep soul lessons, the majority of us, in our human experience, have some or many inner children. From their unhealed consciousness, they continue to affect decisions we take as adults. Just as in school we have lessons to learn, pass and move on from, the earth experience is the same, where we incarnate to assimilate our lessons and understand the purpose of those lessons.

On an esoteric level, lessons and learning may make sense; however, when we are going through traumas on an everyday basis, it is mighty difficult to always remember this. Imagine what will happen when a hurt, troubled child is trying to make choices in relationships or other important decision-making processes. A lot of times, the decisions taken can turn out to be detrimental to the adult, as they are not coming from a place of rationality, practicality or wisdom. Hence, when we make peace with our wounded inner child, we automatically make peace with our adult selves as well and start operating from a holistic place.

Inner children are created for a variety of reasons—because of experiences we go through in our early years, and even when we are in our mother's womb. I will elaborate upon womb healing in a later chapter.

A young child does not really understand adult politics or criticism. A child needs food, shelter, clothing, nurturing, love, touch and a feeling of protection. When these requirements are violated or tampered with, the child goes through deep anguish and can possibly be scarred for life.

In India, the older generations tended to put a premium on fair-skinned children, especially girls. Going by the number of advertisements announcing products to lighten dark skin, the preference for a fair complexion it seems has not completely gone in twenty-first-century India. Well!

So in jest or seriousness, when a dusky young girl repeatedly hears from her family that she is ugly or that no one will marry her because she is dark-skinned, what do you think will happen to the girl's psyche? The answer is obvious.

She will feel worthless, cursed because she was born with dark skin, apologetic for her very existence and full of self-doubt. It's humiliating when her distant relatives or neighbours make fun of her or show 'concern', but when her immediate family says that she is not good enough because she is dark-skinned, then the pain cuts deep—very deep. This girl grows up and turns into a dusky beauty, and when people or men compliment her on her beauty, she finds it very hard to believe (due to childhood rejections) and is wary and judgemental of people who compliment her. She will wonder if they want something from her, if they want to play with her physical body or if they want to cheat her. A simple gesture of appreciation is twisted by her fear and mistrust, and it can take years to cut through the steely cobwebs of feeling worthless and ugly.

My advice would be that as adults, do think twice and be careful of what you say aloud to young children, prepubescent kids and teens. Harsh criticism, comparisons with others, rude comments on their physical appearance, making fun of any disabilities, etc., can damage their psyche and create a negative self-image. Understanding children for who they are and remembering to encourage their positive attributes, rather than pulling them down or threatening them for their failures, creates happier children who grow up to become well-integrated adults.

We have all known people who seem happy and confident on the outside but who have suddenly, one day, exploded emotionally over a mere trifle. To an onlooker, it might seem extreme, this reaction to an innocuous situation, but for the individual, some huge emotional trigger lurking within may have been activated by a seemingly small issue.

As I have mentioned earlier in this chapter, most of our deep emotional triggers are embedded in early childhood or even when we are in our mother's womb. Connected through the umbilical cord, the soul waiting to be born is known to have the capacity to read the mother's emotions and the soul's own feelings while being in the womb. It can pick up vibrations and conversations that are happening in the mother's orbit.

A lady who had a bit of an unhealthy relationship with money once came to me. She would value money so highly that it bordered on stinginess and would always tell her husband, 'Could you give me 5,000 rupees from your money, please?' This 'your' money, 'my' money dichotomy continued to flummox her husband, but she just could not stop.

Somewhat frustrated, she wanted some answers for her weird attitude towards money.

In the session, when I gave the command for her to go back to the root of her issues with money, she went straight to her mother's womb in a soul state, waiting to be born.

As she tuned in and concentrated, this was our conversation:

Client: My mother and father are having a discussion …
Me: Can you hear them?
Client: (after a pause) Yes. They are worried …
Me: What are they worried about?
Client: (longish pause) Money. My parents are scared that they might not have enough money to give me a good education and other things. They are anxious.
Me: (giving her time to process) They are anxious. How is this making you feel?
Client: Very anxious. I am scared too.

I soothed her trauma with a calming technique and bathed her in white light, the highest spectrum of healing light.

As she came out of the womb session and integrated, she was deep in thought and told me that she could clearly hear and feel the anxiety of her parents during their 'lack of money' conversation. Perhaps that was a reason for her stinginess and unhealthy relationship with money, she said.

Incidentally, this lady did well in her studies and professionally too, all on her own steam. She never depended on her parents and worked creatively to earn some money even in her high school days, giving tuition to school students. The session did help her manage her anxiety about money much better, but remnants of the fear of having less money occasionally surfaced.

This is how entrenched emotions from early childhood, or the womb, can create gridlocks that get transmuted into the adult personality as well.

I have worked with very successful professionals who have touched the pinnacle of success in their desired fields but are continuously wracked by self-doubt. 'Am I good enough?' is the question that haunts them. Instead of enjoying their well-earned success, they are constantly in a quagmire of doubt, whipping themselves over what others think of them, what their competitors think of them. It is heart-breaking to see this trauma affect not only the individual but also their partners, spouses and children. In their growing years, this individual would have been made to feel 'not good enough' in a variety of ways—by the family, by friends or by teachers at school. They grew up and decided to show the world their mettle and fought through to rise to the top, but the subconscious worry of 'Am I good enough?' does not allow them to enjoy the fruits of their success.

It can go the other way as well. Another person having the same low confidence can become a drifter all their life, not trying anything for a long period of time, fearing failure, maybe even finding solace in substance abuse or other addictions like sex or gambling.

In dysfunctional families, the chances of children having many 'inner child' fragments are obviously higher. The lack of boundaries in a dysfunctional household can create a damaged personality for life, as children may witness violence, substance abuse, sexual abuse, depression or trauma in their immediate atmosphere.

Roles children tend to play in dysfunctional families

First-born: Aligns to the values and goals of the family. These values and goals could be warped, but the first child tends to be sympathetic to them.

Second-born: Tends to pick up the grief of the parents.

Third-born: Picks up the unresolved conflicts between the parents. This child could try to be the problem-solver and advice-giver or themselves succumb to the same kind of conflicts that are played out between the parents.

Fourth-born: Picks up the unresolved conflicts of the whole family. Can have huge triggers that can create multiple inner children.

Fifth-born: Tends to mimic the first-born, for better or for worse.

The **sixth-born** learns from watching the second-born, while the seventh-born mimics the third-born and the eighth-born looks at the fourth born, and the cycle repeats itself.

The above information has been collated based on my learning and training with inner child expert Patricia Caetano.[3] Most parents are not necessarily aware of this information. However, an astute and observant parent can identify the broad personality quirks and themes of the child.

The predominant personality types

We can all be categorized as archetypes who fall under the various personality types in psychology. These are:

The hero: The eldest child of the family usually takes on the hero personality. This child can turn out to be a high achiever, ambitious and wanting to do things the right way. Their need to be successful can sometimes make them workaholics. All personality types coming from dysfunctional families have low self-esteem.

The caretaker or enabler: This child carries the guilt and shame of the family. They can go to great lengths to keep things secret so that the family is not judged

---

[3] '4 Types of dysfunctional family roles', The Play Therapist, https://www.theplaytherapist.com/dysfunctional-family-roles/.

by the outside world. They can allow themselves or their children to be abused and keep quiet about it. They can have a very painful existence if they remain unhealed. They do not reach out to a therapist easily.

The mascot: This is the clown, the funny child of the family, usually the youngest child. They use humour, self-deprecating or otherwise, to keep family tensions at bay. This child is full of joie de vivre, social and entertaining. They use humour and jokes to put a palliative layer over the negativity in the family. They can feel internally stressed, though, however funny they may appear on the outside.

The peacemaker or placator: They work in tandem with the hero personality, as this child wants to make things better and good for the family. The mascot child can also play the peacemaker role. This child, through speech and behaviour, tries to bring calm resolution to family conflicts. However, in this placatory role, their real needs could flounder.

The scapegoat or rebel: It is usually the second child who acts out this role, but any child who is treated badly or with negative vibes by the family can also behave like this. This child is a horror child for the family—disobedient, angry, frustrated, prone to lying and unpleasant. The family often disregard or are unaware of the fact that through their harsh behaviour, they created this little Frankenstein. Family dynamics are often obtuse and complex, and soon, the scapegoat is blamed for all of the family's troubles. This child grows up with huge deficits in their emotional landscape, which adversely affect their adulthood—and they can turn into rebels without a cause.

The lost child: To cope with dysfunctions in the family, this child creates a fantasy world in their head. While the hero is heroic, the mascot is whipping up fun and the scapegoat is getting blamed, this child is overlooked by the family. The lost child tends to be quiet and passive, preferring to be left alone and not standing out in groups, and hence, they escape the radar of their parents. As an adult, this person tends to be an observer, not engaging much and often standing on the sidelines.

All the above roles can mingle and overlap with each other. But the most important thing to understand is that these childhood roles can get so deeply entrenched in the psyche that they can easily be carried forward into adulthood.

Busy in the grind of daily life, most parents try to do the best for their children—enrolling them in good schools, focusing on extracurricular activities to enhance physical and mental growth, arranging holidays for family bonding and many other things. Then, suddenly, or even over a period of time, some dissonance or behavioural disharmony rears its ugly head and the family is taken aback.

All parents are not trained psychiatrists, psychoanalysts or counsellors, so any sudden 'abnormal' behaviour in their child can throw them off balance and create anxiety. The next step then would be to 'fix' this in whichever way possible. However, in dysfunctional families, where survival itself might be at stake for the adults, the anxiety, anger, fear or other anomalies in the children or young adults might very well go unnoticed.

From my experience, I have seen that adults from dysfunctional families often feel comfortable with toxic co-dependencies. Also, high-stress family systems tend to cause obsessive-compulsive disorders, which, on the face of it, might seem innocuous but have a long-term impact. So do look out if a person you know is eating a lot or dieting in the extreme, if they are cleaning the house compulsively and feel stressed if, for example, a cushion is out of place, if they are exercising a lot or shopping excessively. In fact, any obsessive behaviour is a red flag to look out for.

I have facilitated hundreds of inner child therapy sessions with positive, life-changing outcomes, and my biggest learning in inner child work is that the deepest abandonment issues a child faces occur when they are separated from the biological mother just after birth or soon after birth. That deep-rooted feeling of being unloved, even when they may have loving adoptive parents, is a place of wired energies and non-fulfilment.

Over my many years of practice, I have had around ten clients who were given up for adoption right after birth and did not know anything about their biological parents. Seemingly successful people nurtured by their adoptive parents, they carried a grey pool of depression within. They have tried hard to find their biological parents, especially the mother, and have mostly hit a dead end in their search.

They always carry the question 'Why?'—a wound that continues to bleed pain into their emotional landscape and this supreme abandonment at birth can continue to remain an unhealed trigger in their lives, mostly resulting in them making bad choices.

The umbilical cord: one that can be cut physically but not emotionally

Integrating the inner child after healing all its fragments is joyous. But when one is trying to heal and integrate the inner child of a person abandoned at birth, the process can be very intense and interesting and can throw up sudden challenges.

Here is a story one of my clients shared with me:

'I lived with my adoptive single mother—my adoptive father passed away when I was seven years old—who was extremely strict and bossy and spouted insults at me. She never let me be! So many times a day when I was alone at home during my childhood, I rummaged through the closets and the bookshelves, trying to unearth clues to discover who my real mother was. I always had this inner feeling or intuition that she was someone else! Being an only child and with no extended family or siblings to clarify these growing doubts, I went to the extent of being brave enough to ask my secretive mother who my real mother was!

'My questions were naturally turned down with a yelling, or I was rudely questioned about how I, the child, could have the audacity to question an adult, let alone my mother!

'I was even told that my biological mother was a spoilt brat who wouldn't have cared for me and that, if possible, she would have opted to throw me in the garbage bin, leaving me to live in the dumps had it not been for my adoptive mother, who had taken me in thereafter.

'I was always reminded to be grateful to her, and this was used as a clever, manipulative tactic to get me to do everything she wanted and function like a robot under her orders. Her actions were very hurtful, but I also picked up many good skills; I learnt and explored owing to my experience of living with her.

'The bottomline is that I grew up with the feeling of "I am not good enough" and with absolutely no sense of self. I carried forward my mother's thoughts, beliefs, feelings and behaviour, which had already moulded me. My experiences in life thereafter reinstated the feeling of abandonment, not knowing that I had ended up abandoning myself.

'During this journey of mine, I have realized that I grew up in a household filled with emotionally unavailable family and thus repeated sabotaging patterns in my life, especially in reference to my relationships.

'For the past few years, I have been journaling regularly, putting down on paper my feelings, fears and, in general, my emotions, and have made a list of what I need to work on or seek help for. I read numerous books and subscribed to various programmes related to neuroscience, the body and healing. I had also gone berserk studying, trying to equip myself with various modalities to heal myself.

'When I shared my story with Sabari and mentioned that I was looking to work on various aspects of the mother wound and the father wound, she suggested I book a session with her, saying that this might help as a start.

'During the inner child work, I was guided by Sabari, speaking in her very soothing voice, leading me back to the womb and helping me feel all the emotions my biological mother and I went through together until a while after birth.

'I felt I was in a deep meditative state and started off by being back in the confines of the womb and feeling what my pregnant mother and I had felt when I was inside her.

'I was asked to describe the emotions we were both going through, besides describing the sounds, like my mother's heartbeat and other noises I could hear from within and from outside. There were mixed feelings of comfort, of worry (my mother's), of darkness, of fear, and later, a feeling of hesitancy when it was time to enter the world.

'Sabari guided me, the baby, out into the world. I was being held, then being cleaned, the first cry, being swaddled, being held closely and with love by my real mother. My mother loved me and didn't seem to want to let me go. I could also hear a male voice speaking with her, and what I understood vaguely was that they had to leave me behind. My mother was crying. Later, I was left in a space surrounded by blankness, maybe walls, and I felt alone. Was I crying? Was I alone? Were there cries coming from any other babies? I didn't really know. I looked at the lone child (now as the adult me, as guided by Sabari) and lifted her from her cot, held her close, hugged her tightly and conveyed to her that she was wanted and loved.

'Somewhere in my subconscious, it has soothed me and made me feel good to know that I was loved by my birth mother, and I have overwritten my thoughts and emotions about being unloved and discarded hurtfully by my birth mother. There is a sense of feeling loved, feeling good and feeling free from the negative words said to me as a growing child.

'I am so thankful and grateful to Sabari for taking me through this inner child journey to help me in my

healing journey. It was deeply moving when I thought about it after the session too.'
—*R. Naidu, advertising freelancer, doodle artist, poet*

How to heal your inner child

My honest advice to everyone out there is that inner child healing is deep and deals with entrenched emotional traits and behaviours. So the best gift you can give yourself is to find a trained therapist who is adept in inner child work and go to them. Under guidance, when you can neutralize and heal negative patterns from childhood, you will feel truly liberated as an adult.

If, for some reason, there is no trained therapist near you, then you can do the exercise given below.

- Sit by yourself in a room; make sure you won't be disturbed for forty-five minutes to an hour.
- Focus on your breath. You can play some soothing instrumental music softly. You could try some Buddhist chants if you find them peaceful.
- Allow your physical body to relax completely. Deeply breathe in the safety and comfort of your space. Breathe out any residual anxieties from your mind and body. Do these deep inhalations and exhalations of breath till your body relaxes.

- Guided by the soothing background music, connect with your own self; try and find your own healing space within. Stay with that connection and allow the stillness from your own healing space to flow through your body, deepening your relaxation.
- Now connect with the flowing consciousness that is your mind. Don't try to regulate your thoughts; just try and send the stillness from your body into your mind. Allow your mind to relax.
- Once you feel harmony between your mind and body, imagine, visualize and feel that you are standing in the centre of a circle of golden light. Create that image in your mind and know that you are protected.
- In that circle of divine light, without any stress, allow your mind to gently float back in time to your childhood; keep going further and further back in time till you effortlessly reach a point of dissonance or disturbance in your childhood or early childhood. Connect with that part of you.
- In the circle of golden light, invite that part of you that you just connected with. And also invite all those parts of you, from the youngest to the oldest, who suffered any form of childhood trauma into the protected circle.

Take your time and remember who they all were/are.
- When you feel all those painful parts of you are in the circle, extend both your hands, your palms open, and ask each and every lost part of yours to come and touch you so that you are all connected.
- Using your inner vision, look at all those parts of you and acknowledge their helplessness, their anger, their grief, their dissonance. Let them know you truly understand what they have gone through, because these are the fragmented parts of you. Check with all those parts if they would like to let go of all the past baggage and heal, as you have chosen to heal and raise your vibrations from negativity to positivity. Wait for the answer to pop up in your consciousness.
- If all those parts of you choose to heal, imagine, visualize and feel a warm, streaming golden light falling around all of those parts in the golden circle of light. Let go of the painful childhood memories and behaviours from every cell in your body. Release all into the flowing golden light and ask all the negativity to be taken away from every part of you. Release. Release till you start to feel lighter in mind and body. Using your inner vision, look at all those

parts of you, glowing and healing in the golden light. One by one, go to each one of them and say that you are sorry you could not have been there when they were going through trauma but that you are here now, and never again will they feel alone. With a lot of love and a lot of healing from your heart, integrate the lost parts back into your soul.
- After the integration, take a few moments and see how you feel. If you feel lighter, safer and happier, then integrate all those positive emotions through every layer of your consciousness.
- Exhale deeply and relax.

This exercise can be done as many times as you want, till you genuinely feel happy, lighter and integrated from within.

Once the inner child feels accepted by you, the struggle to feel whole is over. That neglected child's loneliness and pain are over when you embrace them with love. And that acceptance will deeply enrich your life.

'We nurture our creativity when we release our inner child. Let it run and roam free. It will take you on a brighter journey.'

—Serina Hartwell

Chapter 5
Going Deeper into the Subconscious Mind

'The conscious mind may be compared to a fountain playing in the sun and falling back into the great subterranean pool of subconscious from which it rises.'

—Sigmund Freud

Experiencing change by embracing the truth

The subconscious mind, as an adjective, is—'existing in the mind but not immediately available to consciousness'.

And as a noun, it is—'the mental activities just below the threshold of consciousness'.

Both the above definitions are from the Merriam-Webster dictionary. This was a dictionary I loved reading as a child, in search of new words and particularly interested in their pronunciation.

Words can cast spells; they can hold one spellbound or emotionally wreck one's life. Words are powerful, as they penetrate and can reside in the subconscious mind for an eternity.

As regression therapists, we work with the subconscious mind. Of course, in our sessions there is an interplay between the conscious, the subconscious and the superconscious minds, but the subconscious mind is the most important place of revelations.

We work to unveil memories from the subconscious. There are two kinds of memories—modern memory and primitive memory. Modern memory is made up of all our collective experiences and emotions, from the womb to our current age. And primitive memory holds all our past life memories that we have experienced as a soul. The critical mind, or the conscious mind, is like a storage unit or processing unit, where information is stored through the senses.

In our conscious and semi-conscious state of functioning, the mind is always learning through identification and association, and this is how it retrieves and recovers data, transmitting it through the brain to our awareness.

In early childhood, when the critical filter (the ability to understand dangers and good from bad) has not developed yet, the child stores all their experiences directly in the subconscious mind, without even processing them as beneficial or detrimental. The critical mind develops from around eight years onwards; hence, everything the child is feeling physically and emotionally from the womb to eight years of age shapes the modern memory. These feelings are subliminally and deeply entrenched in the psyche, and a lot of healing work is required if this learning is dysfunctional or painful.

I say this often—at Earth school, we learn detachment through attachment. There are, of course, many other schools in the galaxy where we go to learn different things. But at Earth school, the one thing that all human souls have to go through is relationships. Most of us when we reincarnate here choose our families and friends, and we learn life lessons through emotional and physical interactions with other fellow beings. Michael Newton's case studies presented this in his books *Journey of Souls* and *Destiny of Souls*. I have witnessed this multiple times in my Life Between Lives (LBL) work as well.

We experience the warp and weft of the rich tapestry of life woven with feelings of love or hate, respect or disdain, anger or peace, and so many other polarities. Living, as we call it.

If we look at this life from a particular spiritual perspective, then we choose to incarnate to finish our stored karmas and samskaras, while creating current karmas to be lived out in future lives. It might sound a bit complex initially, but it isn't really. Hindus, Jains and Buddhists do believe in different experiences through multiple incarnations, till the soul plays out its maya (illusions) and merges back into the same light it incarnated from.

I use the word light to create the picture of a vibrating high-octane energy, representative of the godhead of all creation as we know it. It could also be a bottomless dark void that was created when space blew up, or an infinitely hot and dense point that expanded to create this universe with a big bang! No one can profess with absolute certainty how the universe was created, but various intelligent theories prevail.

Carl Sagan, the American astronomer, cosmologist and astrophysicist, wrote in his book *Cosmos*:

> 'The Hindu religion is the only one of the world's great faiths dedicated to the idea that the Cosmos itself undergoes an immense, indeed an infinite, number of deaths and rebirths. It is the only religion in which the time scales correspond to those of modern scientific cosmology. Its cycles run from our ordinary day and night to a day and night of Brahma, 8.64 billion years long. Longer than the age of the Earth or the Sun and about half the time since the Big Bang.'

The cosmos, the universe, is so vast that comprehending it is mind-boggling. We can only attempt to 'feel' it through deeply hidden memories within ourselves.

Like a very faint but familiar fragrance. When we remember we are holding universes within ourselves, we understand the meaning of 'Aham Brahmasmi', where the individual soul unites with Brahman, the universal consciousness.

In Hindu mythology, Brahma is also venerated as the creator of the universe.

Here is another favourite quote of mine from Carl Sagan's *Cosmos*:

> 'The nitrogen in our DNA, the calcium in our teeth, the iron in our blood, the carbon in our apple pies were made in the interiors of collapsing stars. We are made of starstuff.'

Now, when this 'starstuff' descends to an atomically heavy plane in heavier human bodies, there are traumas on a moment-to-moment basis—some small, some big, some negligible. Many times, while having to navigate everything Earth school throws at us, we tend to forget we are eternal beings of light and flowing energy.

When the soul light feels dimmed, when the flowing energy feels stuck, it's time to look within and connect with the 'starstuff', the shining and true mettle of our 'beingness'.

The soul might feel bogged down and overwhelmed, and may need a push to start inner soul work. Light workers, healers and trained therapists can guide and extend their help to the struggling soul. Or an honest, wise guru might show that soul the path to the lightness of being.

When my clients come to me, carrying the burden of things and emotions, feeling crushed by the process of living, the first thing I tell them is, 'I laud you for your courage to want to heal yourself. This is the best decision you have taken for yourself.'

It is important to acknowledge the brave step that a person is taking to help themselves.

It is also important to create a nonjudgemental and sacred place in which the client feels comfortable looking into all their vulnerabilities and trusting in the process of healing.

That space is created by being completely honest with the client. The client might wince when the truth is put on the table but will understand it is for their own good, as now the client can own that brutal truth. Once we have the courage to own something, we also have the courage to disown it if it is not for our highest good.

As a therapist, I am empathetic—I listen with full attention and am always kind to people in distress. However, I refrain from sugar-coating life-threatening behavioural issues because it is detrimental to the person who wants to heal. I do believe that 'the truth shall set you free'.

For example, a worried mother might say that the drug addiction her teenage son is going through will surely pass as he grows older—even when the son is selling artefacts and things from the house, she will want to believe that this is just a teenage issue that will go away in some time.

My answer in this situation is, 'Maybe he will sober up in the future, but we don't know if it will surely happen. Most hardcore addiction issues need intense therapy from the root to uncover what void created this addiction.'

Often, messed-up families can create a void within, which young adults want to fill with substance abuse. My conscience does not allow me to tell the distraught mother what she 'wants' to hear.

So be brave and allow yourself to embrace the truth when you are ready to start therapy or any healing, in order to expect and experience change.

The void within

In 2021, a wonderful young man called MJ reached out to me from Amsterdam. I have been facilitating online therapy sessions via Zoom for a long time, and with a little prior preparation with the client, online sessions work out very well.

He had a problem that was taking over his life and he was feeling terribly helpless, not knowing how to deal with it. This is his story in his own words:

'I realized later in adulthood that I suffered from emotional eating, where I would turn to binge eating junk food when I was triggered by anxiety or stressful situations. A confrontational conversation, feeling stressed with a high workload, moments where I felt I wasn't good enough—my instinct was to comfort myself by eating lots of junk food. I would eat two big burgers, huge amounts of fries, a milkshake and icecream in one sitting. I would then feel terrible and physically and mentally sick, but the cycle never ended. It escalated during the Covid-19 pandemic, and I figured how badly this binge eating was affecting my life. I decided I had to break the pattern.

'Sabari helped me access my subconscious mind and helped me identify where it came from. It came from huge fears deep inside my mind. Fears of being judged and not being good enough. Sabari then guided me to neutralize these fears from the root, and after the sessions, I didn't give them much thought. I didn't know if they had worked or not until some weeks later, when I was in a similarly anxious situation, but I naturally found myself not wanting to turn to junk food. It's now been over three years and I haven't had any triggers that have put me back where I was.'

Addictions are not generated in the conscious mind. Their twisted roots are deeply implanted in the psyche, but with patience and sustained healing work, involving the soul's higher mind, addictions can be brought under control and then completely uprooted. The individual's willpower is a big catalyst in initiating change and then holding on to that positive change for life.

In trying to deal with trauma, unknowingly, some might tend to create self-sabotaging patterns or a cycle of negative situations. When we start believing our own self-created stories that we are not good enough, not worthy enough, not physically attractive enough, we inevitably create negative patterns in our lives, consciously unable to join the dots as to why a gloomy pattern keeps repeating itself.

Change is not for everyone

Here is a case study of repeated negative patterns.

My domestic worker (I will call her X for the sake of this exercise) has been told by everyone who knows her that she should leave her husband. X was widowed soon after her first marriage, when her husband died from alcoholism. She suddenly became a single mother with a little baby girl. Not having any family support, she struggled to make ends meet and eventually re-married. She had two children from this second/current marriage too. She makes sure her eldest daughter is educated in an English-medium school. The current husband works sporadically and has made enough money to build a house in a nearby town. However, his relationship with his wife is tumultuous, filled with jealous rages and physical beatings. Her well-wishers keep urging her to leave him, but she stays on.

One day, the husband made sexual moves on X's preteen daughter. This was unbearable for X. She raved, ranted, threatened and threw her husband out of the house. He came back soon enough, but their landlady wisely gave the daughter a small room so that she didn't have to sleep in the same room as the rest of the family.

The stepfather, though, continued to have a lecherous eye on the girl. Long story short, one night, when threatened with a police case, he drank some poison, and people informed X that her husband was sprawled in the middle of the road, unconscious. At 2 a.m., there was no immediate help or car available to take him to a hospital, so she begged the fire brigade to help, and they helped her.

The no-gooder husband lived, but she went through endless police station visits since it was a suicide attempt. X thought of leaving him, hired a lawyer and faced the song and dance of a long legal process. People helped her, counselled her, encouraged her to leave the lout. But she decided not to leave.

Her daughter is a teenager now, a bright kid who does well in school and is her mother's kindred spirit.

I earnestly asked X, 'Why aren't you leaving? Do you know how difficult it is for your daughter to live with a sexual predator lurking around?'

She said, 'I am keeping a hawk's eye on my husband. If he slips one more time, I will leave him.'

We looked at each other with wry smiles. We both knew she wouldn't take that step towards her freedom. The cycle of karma will continue, and the healing will flap its wings beyond the stage doors, just waiting for her to walk into the spotlight and claim her rightful place on the stage of life.

This kind of story is not limited to just X. Across the world, this story is played out an incalculable number of times. The beatings and abuse may be physical, the welts and bruises fade away with time, but the soul shrinks into a darkness where pinpoints of any light feel like a violation, and all that one desires in that acute tiredness is to shut one's eyes. Shut the 'beingness' to receive no help, no healing, no succour. Wrapped in blackness, just awaiting the sweet kiss of death. The final escape.

Healing ourselves is a lifelong venture of letting go of baggage that mentally and emotionally wears us down. We also have to be extremely mindful that we do not keep regressing to the past. Once we have thrown the baggage out, we definitely don't need to bring back any heaviness from the past.

To continue to travel light, do use all the tools and techniques that you learn during your healing/therapy sessions. These are gifts, and you should use them continuously, on your own, not to slip into a rut again.

However, life can be full of complexities, and in this long journey of living, if newer problems crop up that one is not able to resolve within oneself, please seek help again. If problems remain unresolved and fester inside, they tend to start impacting our physical body energies in many different ways—as constant aches and pains, allergies, feelings of deep tiredness, an inability to focus and even autoimmune disorders. The list of maladies can be long, so there is no need to overwhelm your emotional balance.

In the words of Mahatma Gandhi, 'Your beliefs become your thoughts, your thoughts become your words, your words become your actions, your actions become your habits, your habits become your values, your values become your destiny.'

So, fellow travellers, believe that you can travel light to wonderful ethereal and non-ethereal destinations of your choice.

Begin your healing journey

Here are a few simple exercises that will help you connect with your subconscious mind and loosen the knots of repetitive loops.

1. **Meditation**
   The subconscious mind is a churning ocean of fervent emotions, with choppy waves of traumas and afflictions.

   One needs to understand this deep ocean a bit and calm it significantly so that we are not tossed around by these monstrous waves and feel imbalanced.

   A deep state of focus and surrender of control, which can be achieved in a meditative state, helps considerably in maintaining one's mental balance.

Meditation is actually a natural state of being. When we have to make a major decision, we tend to ponder over and reflect on the decision so that we do not make the wrong judgement. We meditate on it. When we are doing or creating something we love deeply, we go into a quiet, joyous state of concentration. That too is a state of meditation.

Many people tell me that they meditate by focusing on their breath. This is a difficult meditation for beginners; even practising yogis take years to reach a state where they can 100 per cent focus on their breath without any distractions. It takes a while to get there; hence, I also hear from people who only do breath meditation that their mind starts wandering often.

The best way to start a meditation practice is to listen to a guided meditation, in which a voice guides you into a soothing turiya state of surrender. All you have to do is listen to the guidance that is helping the chattering mind reach a quiet, meditative state.

If you search for 'guided meditation for relaxation' on YouTube, many suggestions will come up. Select a thirty-minute guided meditation to begin with, and make sure to choose a voice that you like. Listen to it at least once a day. Once the mind's chatter diminishes and the surrender to calm and stillness gets better and better, in the post-meditative space, where you feel connected to the self, gently reflect on the repeated negative patterns in your life, without any judgement.

See what your mind throws up as you reflect on the issues. Hear what your inner voice is whispering to you. Allow all its messages to surface and pay attention to them.

As your inner voice gains strength and the messages get clearer and stronger, see if you can join the dots for yourself. What unhealed triggers are making you repeat self-harming patterns, if any? With the inner knowing that is surfacing in your meditative state, can you muster the wisdom to let go and end these repeated patterns by healing the triggers that cause them?

If the answer is yes, heal yourself and allow yourself to be free from things that do not help your growth as a being.

2. **Therapy and healing**
Many a time, we are too close to our own dramas and lose the ability to be dispassionate. When someone comes to seek our advice, we tend to be objective and can genuinely give some great advice to help resolve a situation. However, when it comes to advising ourselves, we tend to dither, caught in our own quagmire of emotions, and this can make us feel directionless and confused.

In such a situation, rather than keeping quiet, it can be helpful to talk to a trusted friend or family member. Go to someone who is caring and nonjudgemental.

If there is no friend or family member you wish to talk to, find a good subconscious mind therapist or healer, who can help you resolve any repeated negative patterns. A professional who knows how to guide you, without imposing on you, can definitely help you heal with therapeutic tools and techniques, and they can also guide you to connect with your higher self, since when all is said and done, the answers lie within us.

Faith gives one the biggest impetus to explore and help rejuvenate the self. Faith in anything—people, hobbies, spiritual explorations, enriching conversations, time travel of the mind and to physical places, creativity and discoveries. Try to allow the soul to soar and not to shrink.

Chapter 6
Regressing to Past Lives

'I died as a mineral and became a plant, I died as plant and rose to animal, I died as animal and I was Man. Why should I fear? When was I less by dying?'

—**Rumi**

According to the Buddha's teachings, all beings go through cycles of birth and rebirth, ending this reincarnation process only through spiritual enlightenment.

The Buddha's disciples wrote about his various incarnations in the Jataka tales, which I devoured as a child. I was agog with curiosity, reading about the Buddha-to-be going through various incarnations, from murderers to sages to royalty, even animals and different metaphysical beings. The tales sport an array of interesting characters, from the wise to the wily.

Each story is a lesson the Buddha-to-be had to learn on his path to enlightenment and Buddhahood. He was much like all of us—a spiritual being having a human incarnation. We are here to learn our chosen lessons; we can choose to finish them over lifetimes and are always seeking enlightenment to be freed from the eternal cycle of pain and karmic debts.

In Buddhism, Jainism and Hinduism, karma is an important word in the concept of reincarnation, leading towards mukti, or release from the cycle of birth and death. The Buddha's teachings on karma and rebirth are the core of the Buddhist religion.

Positive actions augur positive consequences and negative ones, negative consequences. These consequences are not limited to one lifetime but span millions of lifetimes. We finish karmas and make new karmas, and we continue this process till all our karmas are resolved when we receive enlightenment of the mind and soul.

The Buddha taught that existence is a continuous cycle of birth, death and rebirth known as samsara. The unfinished karmas propel these cycles of birth and rebirth till nirvana (enlightenment) of thought and action is achieved. The Buddha inspired his disciples to develop awareness, mindfulness and ethical conduct to generate positive karma and ultimately attain liberation from the cycle of rebirth.

Over the years, many people have asked me if there is life after death and if souls choose multiple rebirths. My answer to both questions has always been 'Yes'.

Yes because not only have I seen many, many past lives of mine, but also I have facilitated over 3,000-plus PLR sessions till date, where my clients have seen, felt and discovered their own past lives.

Then, of course, there are the books and the writers of those books who themselves have had and facilitated past life experiences for others.

I first read Dr Brian Weiss's *Many Lives, Many Masters* in junior college. In the book, Catherine's recall of her myriad past lives, which Dr Weiss inadvertently led her to, and the use of his skills as a psychiatrist/hypnotherapist to help heal her traumatic past life memories enable Catherine to become a happier person. This book had an indelible effect on my mind. Born a Hindu, never did I think we live only one life. The Jataka tales, stories of Lord Krishna in his different avatars, mythology I heard from my grandparents—all of these sealed the idea that we reincarnate over lifetimes. *Many Lives, Many Masters* was just another confirmation of the same.

However, what fascinated me was the incredible healing that happened to Catherine through her PLR sessions. Her life changed completely for the positive, and it was fascinating how Dr Weiss held the space for her through her other lives narrations and dexterously guided Catherine's soul into deep healing and wellness.

Dr Brian Weiss's next book, *Only Love Is Real*, sealed my fate! I read it in the first semester of college, going through young relationship angst myself, and this book turned my consciousness upside down. Written beautifully, Elizabeth and Pedro's love story over lifetimes tore into me like a rip tide. It gave me the hope that relationships do not end with finality in a lifetime, that the dance of love is danced many times over in many different lifetimes and forms. This knowledge made me a little forlorn initially, but as I let it seep through every layer of my consciousness, it also liberated my mind in a strange way. I decided that if I fall in love, I will love with my entire soul, and if the relationship breaks, then so be it—maybe the guy will show up in some life or the other, looking like Johnny Depp! The Johnny Depp story is shared later in this chapter itself.

I read *Many Lives, Many Masters* in 1989, not even imagining in my wildest dreams that in July 2010, I would be learning PLR at Dr Weiss's training at the Omega Institute in upstate New York. It was exhilarating to be in the same room as Dr Weiss, the man who shone light on many understandings in my consciousness, which I gleaned from his books.

In that training, I soaked it all in. I learnt, unlearned, said 'Wow' many times under my breath and totally surrendered to all the experiences in class and out of class in client–therapist practice sessions with fellow students. After classes, I would go for a swim in the lake at Omega, and the refreshing water calmed me and helped push my boundaries in a non-stressful way, and this, in turn, encouraged me to learn more. Unknown to me then, my cellular memories were tingling with excitement, happy I was finally aligning with my old selves as a shaman, a healer, a guardian of crystals, a philosopher, a teacher and a warrior.

I was so comfortable that, physically, I felt as if I were walking into class in my old, all-accepting nightdress.

In one of the group sessions, Dr Weiss was inducting the whole class into a past life experience, opening up neuropathways in the subconscious mind, and during this class, I had a surreal, spiritually profound experience. The experience is difficult to describe through mere words, but I will try my best to explain what happened to me that afternoon.

It was a post-lunch session, the big hall was in shadows and Dr Brian Weiss had started his induction into a past life journey. All of us students were lying on our floor mats with our eyes closed, following our teacher's hypnotic voice.

I went into a state of calm and quiet following the guided induction, but after a while, I was in a deep somnambulist state, where there were no voices, no sounds, no floor mats, no body, just a tranquil hush.

I felt the loving presence of Meher Baba, one of my close spiritual guides. Meher Baba picked me up in his arms; my spirit body felt like a little baby, cradled securely in his arms. And then the journey began. Oh boy!

Meher Baba and I floated through a gleaming, star-studded, purplish and velvety space; it was dark but shimmering with an unseen light. I saw galaxies like star-spangled passages and floated over them. I was experiencing the deep void of space, yet space felt airy and light, and a deep, enriching hum surrounded me. I felt joy in every pore of my body and a thrum—notes of music were emanating from me—and I was laughing and smiling in the deepest recognition that I belonged here.

This space travel was Meher Baba's gift to me, reminding me where we truly belong, giving credence to the fact that we are all spiritual beings having a human experience.

Honestly, I am unable to do justice to that phantasmagorical, intensely sacred experience with these written words. Writing comes from our subconscious mind, but as I write now, I fall short of words because my astral experience was beyond the outer limits of my mind then. Yet I carry this experience so lightly, so easily and naturally within me—transformed till the day of my physical death in this lifetime.

No, this wasn't my kundalini rising or any physical thing like that. This experience can only happen when a guru guides you into this, or when a portal opens in your consciousness and you feel the vastness of your own existence.

Yuvraj Kapadia, founder and CEO of EKAA Integrated Clinical Hypnotherapy Foundation and International Academy of Life, who was one of my teachers in hypnotherapy training, once shared the account of a seemingly unbelievable PLR session.

He said that his client, a smart young woman who worked in an international hotel chain, came for a PLR session.

Kapadia's client went back to a past life, where she followed Gautama Buddha's teachings and was deeply entrenched in Buddhism. As a facilitator, Yuvraj was trying to delve deeper into the past life of this young woman, when she sat up on the therapy couch, eyes still closed, and bent backwards so that her head touched her spine.

I still remember Yuvraj saying how shocked he was at seeing this difficult yogic contortion. Before he could say anything, the young woman said: 'I am a Bodhisattva.'

In Buddhism, a Bodhisattva is one who is walking on the path towards Buddhahood or an awakening of the soul. A Bodhisattva's vow is also to help other beings find their awakening.

Over the years, while facilitating past life sessions, I have experienced that regressing clients to unresolved experiences in their past lives and healing those unresolved points has helped them completely recover from physical, mental and emotional issues in their current life. Once those cellular memories of trauma are healed and neutralized, the person is able to integrate and heal their current life malaises. I have seen this to be especially true for medical conditions like migraine, asthma, psoriasis and unexplained aches and pains; in my sessions, 90 per cent of these conditions tend to have unhealed roots in an earlier past life.

Often, relationship issues can have unhealed scars from past lives and be carried forward vibrationally as cellular memories for resolution in current lives. Past life regression sessions open a window to these scars from the past, and with the client's inner knowing and the guidance of the therapist, they can reach a deeper understanding in this life, freeing them from lifelong interpersonal clashes and dissonances.

In many present life crises, healing can come from resolving past life issues. For example, in current life crisis situations, when a client cannot find an answer as to which direction they need to take, I ask them if they would like to set up this intent: 'Which past life in my soul journey is relevant to this current life? What wisdom that I gained in a past life can I use in my current life?' Sometimes deep wisdom comes from a very relevant situation that the soul has already navigated, and the client, by revisiting that 'been there, done that' situation, understands how to solve the current life crisis.

Your dream will find you

Jeanette is a vibrant American woman who has been associated with India for quite a while. She created and nurtured Padukas Artisans, a handicrafts workshop made up of local artisans, mainly from the village of Ganeshpuri, Maharashtra, and is also an adviser/volunteer at the Om Gagangiri Maharaj Aashirwadit Trust. Jeanette has a PhD in Jungian and archetypal psychology, and when we met, she was looking for some answers.

'A fairly intense rumbling in our consciousness kept making itself known—we could no longer continue to manage a small retreat centre in one of India's beautiful pilgrimage sites, known as the Gurudev Siddha Peeth.

'My husband, Dewa, and I felt a need to move on and leave the home and work that we had been managing for over twelve years. It takes a bit of courage to leave a home within which one has become comfortable. So I thought of calling Sabari Chakraborty for a past life regression session to see if I could get some insight into what was emerging in our minds and hearts.

'In Sabari's beautiful home in Mumbai, she led me to her office, where she conducts very personal regressions into one's thoughts, feelings and memories. With little discussion about why I was asking for a regression, Sabari led me into an altered state, where images appeared in my mind.

'She guided me to look at my feet, and I immediately saw old sandals worn by a man, possibly in some desert in the Middle East. She asked me to look at my clothes and my body. I realized that I was an old man, with dishevelled, worn clothing and unkempt dreadlocks from living as a desert nomad.

'Sabari asked me to look around the place I was in. I saw that I was one of very few people left after marauding bandits had burnt down our nomadic home, killed our men, taken our women and left only a few disabled elders and orphaned children. I felt that everyone left behind was in shock from having witnessed the horrifying event of having our homes destroyed and our loved ones either killed or kidnapped.

'It soon became obvious that I was the most competent and resourceful person among those who were left. I realized there was no logical reason to stay here, where there was no food, no water, no shelter from the harsh elements of the desert. Our only solution to save ourselves was to move to a safer location where there might be provisions.

'I was suddenly inspired by the thought that we had extended family living near a body of water, many days' journey away. I imagined that we might at least be able to find help and resources to survive along the waterside. It would be a long, hard journey, and not all of us would necessarily make it out alive. But we could not stay where we were, since we would obviously perish from the harsh environment or at the hands of more scavenging bandits.

'I cannot remember if we finally made it to the waterside village. Maybe we did and found it hospitable.

Maybe I did not actually see myself getting there. But one thing was very clear. We had to move on. I had to trust my instincts to move to a possibly better location, sight unseen. I had to lead our band on.

'Coming out of the deep regression, I became clear about my need to leave what was once comfortable and strike out into the unknown. I knew I had to follow my instincts. It was an overwhelming kind of knowing!

'Within a month of the regression, my husband and I were faced with the dissolution of our comfortable lifestyle and home. One day, it was all dissolved, just like being ripped apart by cruel bandits. But because of the regression I went through, I felt forewarned of the destruction that was occurring. I also had a sense that a new adventure was unfolding even though it was unclear. I faced the challenge of quitting our job and home with the knowledge that our old way of life had ended, just like the painful images of the regression. It was time to face the situation head-on and move to a new location, one that might be bountiful, like living near an oceanside.

'Our new home did not appear immediately. We faced more dissolution of other temporary homes and eventually even had to leave Mother India. We travelled throughout the USA for almost a year, looking for a new home, yet nothing seemed to call us.

'Three years after the regression, we found our new home in Mexico, alongside the most beautiful freshwater lake, Lake Chapala. The 420-square-mile lake emanates a sense of richness and bounty, and the feeling of being blessed by the Divine Mother. The town is full of like-minded people who are comfortable living in an exotic foreign land and enjoying what life offers moment to moment. In some way, this new home perfectly matches the image from the regression of travelling months and maybe years in the desert to discover a place along a body of water that is receptive and conducive to forming new friendships and living a life of beauty and joy.

'Having the past life images in my mind of being forced to create a new life kept me encouraged to take the necessary steps in this life. I am so grateful to Sabari for lovingly guiding me to a deep inspiration to trust the process that was unfolding, no matter how long it would take.'

Jeanette now lives in Mexico with Dewa, in the ashram of their guru, and they are immensely joyful.

In 2013, a lovely woman named Rupali visited my clinic. Rupali had married into a wealthy business family, and even though she had been married for four years or so, she was unable to conceive. She found me through a friend and contacted me to seek some help.

With unsaid pressures from a traditional family and the fear of her biological clock ticking away, Rupali was seeking a deeper answer to why she was unable to conceive, because medically she was declared fit and fine.

In our first session, I could sense an underlying sadness and some amount of stress regarding her planned motherhood, which was not exactly going to plan. Rupali was open to figuring out if the problem was due to some energy dis-balance that she might have been creating unknowingly. During the conversation, she asked if a PLR session would help. I said, 'Sure, I am happy to explore the root of this issue with you.' We scheduled a session, and Rupali left.

Here is Rupali's story in her own words:

'When I went to meet Sabari, I did not know what to expect, but from deep within, I knew that I wanted to explore the reason for my childlessness and see if there were some things that were beyond my understanding. We talked about me being under pressure when it came to motherhood. And even though everything was okay, I was just not conceiving. Sabari said that the root of the issue could be in the past—either in early childhood, in the womb or maybe in some past life. I was open to exploring, and if there was a cause of this somewhere else, then I felt eager to understand what that might be.

'As we started the session to regress to the root of why I was unable to conceive, pretty quickly I went back to a past life where I was a Bedouin woman in a hijab, living in a mud hut in a desert. The place felt like current-day Afghanistan or near it, an arid region.

'I was in an unhappy marriage, and though my husband wanted a child, I did not want to be a mother. So when I conceived and figured I was having a baby, I contacted a midwife and secretly had an abortion. I just did not want to be a mother, especially in a bad marriage.

'Through tears running down my face, I told Sabari that soon my husband found out about my abortion, and he was furious. He cursed me, saying that I would never be able to be a mother ever again. It was an extremely traumatic time and I felt completely helpless.'

When I guided her away from that devastating life and asked Rupali to look down at that life from the higher place of her soul mind or higher consciousness, she said, 'I am so sorry for what I did. I should have talked to my husband; maybe he would have understood. I am sorry, so sorry ...' Her pain was deep and intense.

I then initiated the journey of this soul's forgiveness. Rupali's soul mind went back to that life as I invoked and requested the angels of white light to guide Rupali's soul to that moment when her husband had cursed her with childlessness. Protected by the light of the angels of white light, Rupali begged her husband's soul for forgiveness and admitted the huge mistake her soul had committed. There was a healing exchange between the two souls of husband and wife, and finally the husband's soul told Rupali, 'I forgive you completely, and I will come back to you as your son in your next birth.'

It was an emotional, poignant moment in my clinic. I used all the healing protocols to neutralize and rewrite Rupali's soul memories of her most immediate past life and magnified the healing to wash away residual negative feelings.

Rupali and I talked quietly about what had just unfolded, and she understood it was a past journey and that it need not affect her current life conditions. In this life, she had a supportive husband and they both wanted to have children.

We went back to our lives, doing what we do, and the session was filed and put away. After about seven months, Rupali called to tell me she was expecting twins. She was happy. For me, it was another reminder that when healing happens at the root of an unresolved issue, our souls are set free from the shackles that hinder our lives physically, emotionally or mentally.

When I asked Rupali to write about her session in her own words, I was reminded that her husband in her past life had promised to come back as her son in her current lifetime. So I checked with Rupali. Rupali had given birth to twins—two boys. When asked about her sons, she said she had a great relationship with them, a deep connect especially with the younger son. To me, this is obviously a bond that has lasted lifetimes.

Twin flames and twin souls

It is fascinating to me, as a regression therapist, how group soul members reincarnate with each other in multiple lifetimes, helping each other learn and complete valuable soul lessons and move on.

Incarnations with group soul members are like doing class projects together, each member playing a designated role to bring the project to fruition. We might not know this on a conscious level, but in our superconscious mind, we have already created a blueprint of our lives before being born. Unknowingly, yet knowingly, we aspire to reach detachment through attachments, the various souls playing 'good cop, bad cop' in our lives only to aid us in working through our lessons, and we, in turn, helping them with theirs.

On the other hand, incarnations with twin flames and twin souls tend to throw up interesting, dramatic lifetimes. Lifetimes of great healing, great loss, unfulfilled dreams—a medley of karmas that the twins choose to finish at a fast pace, because when twin flames incarnate together, that lifetime is a very special one.

Twin flames and twin souls are two distinct spiritual concepts, though they are often used interchangeably.

Twin flames are equally divided parts of the same soul, created from the same divine spark. They are considered a rare and intense soulmate connection, where the two individuals feel an overwhelming pull and connection to one another, even if they are not necessarily in a romantic relationship.

Twin souls, on the other hand, are considered spiritual counterparts or kindred spirits. They may not have the same level of acute soul connection as twin flames, but they do share a deep and meaningful spiritual bond. Twin souls can be in platonic, familial or romantic relationships.

While there are similarities between the two concepts, the key distinction is the intensity and spiritual depth of the connection, as I mentioned earlier. Twin flames are a more profound and fated pairing, while twin souls have a strong spiritual affinity that does not feel so fatalistic.

The twin flame is the other half of a soul that split and separated to acquire its own learnings and experiences. Usually, twin flames veer between masculine and feminine energy frequencies, the warrior and the nurturer. One split half may choose more masculine soul signatures and the other more feminine signatures. When they choose to cross paths in a particular lifetime, they decide who will be the nurturer and who the warrior, based on the life learnings both will help each other to attain. Twin flames do not come together often, even though the halves might pine for 'the one' in the lives where they either don't incarnate together or just touch each other's lives fleetingly. Even those fleeting brushes are transformative in some way or the other, and the soul does not forget that encounter.

Many a time, a short-lived relationship and consequent break-up can linger on in our hearts for a lifetime, even though we have moved on with other partners to other environments. We might even find it strange that the memory of an ephemeral encounter feels firmly lodged in the psyche. If that happens, surely your twin flame and you brushed against each other to kindle the eternal flame of your oneness.

How twin flames meet on the physical plane is always sudden, unexpected and 'coincidental'. But one immediately recognizes a twin flame as one's soul memory gets activated, and it feels like you are looking at a piece of your heart. The reflection of you is in the gaze of that 'stranger'. The heart soars, every cell tingles and you feel intensely alive at this recognition.

What follows the first encounter could be heartbreaking, life-changing, spiritually uplifting, gut-shattering, short-lived, long-lived, but it always leads to a healing and acceleration of spiritual growth. Twin flame incarnations do not happen in every lifetime. A twin flame shows up for important lessons in a difficult life, where the showing up could be for a short or a nominally longer period of time. However, when a twin flame is around for practically the whole lifetime, it means that the two halves must perform some incredible work, usually for the larger good of society or a large group of souls. Then they harmoniously support each other to contribute to the cause that is larger than themselves.

I accidentally found out during my first LBL session that my husband and I are twin flames. Well, accidental it is not—I was given this knowledge when my guides wanted me to know.

I went on to see multiple past lives; whenever we chose a lifetime together, my twin flame would have a premature death, leaving me to have profound experiences of healing through the grief and loss. I would learn detachment through attachment. As I experienced those sessions, it was intensely painful, but in a magical way, it was also light and liberating. I felt an enriching sense of gain through the loss.

A life of love, loss and belonging

Here is an account of my session with therapist Dr Ameeta Thacker in 2011, where I was first introduced to a twin flame experience in a past lifetime:

'I am a teenage girl, fifteen or sixteen years old, looking out of the window at a somewhat arid landscape with some Mediterranean trees, like palms and gnarled olives. I am smiling, mostly for no reason, my heart feeling joyful and light. I am wearing a loose embroidered dress and have my hair in two plaits that run down both my shoulders.

'I live in a village of mud houses, where we follow the religion of Islam. I have girlfriends with whom I exchange jokes, take part in the local gossip and enjoy festivities. I do not have a father; I live with my mother, who stitches clothes and does some embroidery work by hand. I am a curious, happy teenager.

'After anchoring me in that atmosphere, my therapist guided my subconscious mind to go to a very important event in that lifetime. A milestone, even.

'I am in a desert, my heart full of joy and excitement, as my fiancé is visiting me. I am smiling, and we are teasing each other and cavorting on two beautiful horses. My horse is white, and his horse is bigger and jet black. He is an expert horseman, but I am not bad either. We are showing off our riding skills in a golden sandy desert. I can see the pinkish-red sun hovering just above the horizon. We are so in love and thrilled to be with each other.

'My therapist, Ameeta, did some quick deepening and asked me to focus deeper and look into the eyes of my fiancé, the man I love so much.

'Oh my god! He looks like Johnny Depp—and his eyes … his eyes … he is Indranil.'

Indranil, my husband in my current life, my lover, friend, partner over multitudinous lifetimes. I was so overwhelmed by this soul recognition that tears began pouring down my cheeks, my voice lost in the depths of bottomless, fathomless love. Beyond love. A searing understanding of how strong the vibrations of connectedness are between two souls, mirroring each other. And at that point, I still did not know that he is my twin. That knowing came much later. Back to the session:

'Golden, it's golden all around. The sun is bathing everything in its golden light. While viscerally feeling that golden early dusk, through my knowing, it came to me that my fiancé is a rising lieutenant in the Ottoman Empire's army. He is brave and shooting fast up the ranks and the sultan is fond of him. He loves me; he is from a neighbouring village and wants to marry me. The geographical area, I felt, was Damascus. My fiancé comes whenever he can from his army duties to meet me. We always meet in the desert, where there is privacy.

'Suddenly, I sense some tension in my fiancé. From being carefree and light, his head sharply turns to face the horizon, and his gaze becomes piercing. I turn my head too; there is nothing. But rather quickly I see ...

'There are soldiers. Soldiers who are coming towards us. I am feeling worried now. He is telling me to quickly hide. I do not want to leave him. No. But he tells me to go now. Hide.

'I am steering my horse away; I can see a sand dune ahead. I gallop towards the dune and quickly hide behind it. Something is wrong ... My heart is pounding.

'Then the session turns into waves of indescribable grief. I see the soldiers, and from their red and silver attire, I know they are from the royal army. My fiancé is trying to run away, but they catch him, surround him and attack him with long, pointed spears. He falls from his horse, and the soldiers brutally lance him to death. I watch as they pick up his bloodied, lifeless body and take it away with them. At that moment, I turn to stone. I lose consciousness. When I become conscious, the desert is cold and it is a moonlit night. Gathering my senses, I see my horse, silent, standing next to me. I come out from my hiding place; in the distance, I see a black shadow moving aimlessly. My fiancé's beloved horse.

'The following fifteen minutes are a jumble, and I remember not speaking much in the session but feeling the deepest gut-wrenching grief, with all my cellular memories jangling with the remembrance of the loss of my twin flame. The session continues.

'I'm unable to come out of my shock and am like the living dead. My mother passes away, and after many years, with the support of the village, I slowly become somewhat functional.

'I start making gold jewellery, small earrings and pendants, by hand. I can't ever feel any emotions in that life, instead I just focus on my work. I go to the palace to meet the king to seek justice for my fiancé's murder. A kind, high-ranking official meets me. In the session, I see myself on my knees in front of him, crying. The official says, "I am genuinely sorry for what happened. Your fiancé was murdered because some people hated his popularity and the fact that the king liked him!"

'Nothing changes; my heart is stone. I just breathe. Cut to the final moments before my physical death. I am lying in bed, not feeling well. I am probably in my sixties, with women and other villagers around me. I sense a golden light in the room and hear words foreign to me. But immediately, I recognize that they are Arabic words, holy words.

'There is a woman, clad in a head-to-toe black robe, sitting by my bedside, saying the words in a reverent tone. In a flash of recognition, the knowing comes to me that she is Shabana, a great cook who had cooked for my family till she left Mumbai and went back to her village in Uttar Pradesh.

'I still remember my little shock in the session at this recognition. Gratitude followed the initial nanosecond of shock. Shabana (the lady who read the Kalima in that past life) nurtured me by cooking for me in my life as Sabari, even if it was for a short while, and she also held sacred space for me and guided my soul to the afterlife in my life in Damascus.'

We are all connected as souls, which we forget again and again in our human and hybrid incarnations. Indeed, school lessons are about war and peace, destruction and reconstruction, love and hate, dreams and nightmares. An ever-changing matrix, aiding our consciousness to keep growing and finally merge back with the universal consciousness from where we spawned. Not from 'dust to dust' but from light to light we go.

Later, during my first LBL session, I received the information that Indranil is my twin flame. In retrospect, the intensity of loss I felt in losing my fiancé in the Damascus life made sense to me.

In fact, when I was in high school, I had seen a picture of the golden-domed Great Mosque of Damascus in a travel magazine, and immediately my heart yearned to go there. I visualized that place many times over and felt a tingling of anticipation every time. I did some research and found out that the Ottoman Empire's imperial realm included Damascus and Syria too, between the early sixteenth and early eighteenth centuries. And when I first visited the Topkapi Palace in Istanbul, there was a huge rush of recognition as I wandered around. Was it here that I came to beg for justice for my murdered fiancé? I still don't know for sure, and yet it felt so emotional. I kept asking my husband, the fiancé in my Damascus life, 'Do you feel like you have been here before? Isn't this place familiar?' Indranil said, 'No, it doesn't seem familiar to me.' I let it pass.

I have seen some more past lives where we twins incarnated together, and in the majority of those lives, my twin either died an unnatural death or moved away. In this life too, Indranil and I were college sweethearts, but he broke up with me after college, shattering my heart, and moved on. Funnily, he is the one who tried to stay connected with me over the years, after the break-up, through common friends. I didn't bother to keep tabs on him too much, though ... Hadn't he broken my heart?

Yet we came back together in this life, eighteen years after our break-up, to live together, get married, build a life holding each other's hands. The love had gone nowhere, it seems.

In my spiritual journeys, through my esoteric wanderings and by listening to my spirit guides, I realized that in this lifetime, both Indranil and I chose to come together and stay together because we had chosen to do work that is bigger than our human selves, and the twins had to support each other in bringing this work to fruition. This massive knowledge download was overwhelming at first, but then something I accepted with limitless gratitude.

I have learnt that in numerous incarnations, I have vibrated with the male essence and Indranil has vibrated with a more feminine core. I have mostly been a warrior-healer and he a nurturer. This is how a twin flame combination works perfectly. Both parts shapeshift, going through their personal journeys, but come back together in mellifluous harmony when required.

I decided to write in detail about this past life session because it is possible that many of you are having intense, deeply meaningful past life journeys, and maybe sometimes, you are falling a little short of deciphering their true relevance to your soul cycle. I continue to seek every day, and maybe my in-depth account of what emerged from my seeking, in just one regression session, will inspire you to look deeper between the layers and give you the courage to ask more questions and listen to the answers without any judgements.

Is it possible to regress to a past life without any therapist intervention?

Yes, it is possible. I have heard of numerous people having spontaneous regressions to their past lives and getting important information from those forays. They are not avatars but regular people triggered into a regression by a catalyst. The catalyst can be physical, emotional or spiritual.

Yogis, of course, use deep meditation techniques to glean spiritual knowledge from their past lives and use it to enhance their spiritual odysseys.

If you wish to experience a self-induced PLR, here is an exercise you can follow:

- Sit comfortably in a semi-dark room; you could have a soft, warm light on or even a candle.
- Do some relaxing inhalations and exhalations till your body feels loose and light. Allow your mind to just be, only focused on your gentle breathing.
- If you choose to, play some meditative chants or music in the background at low volume. Once

your body and mind feel genuinely relaxed, say the word 'love' to yourself. Repeat it gently to yourself a few times, maybe even saying 'my greatest love', 'the most important love', and letting go. Without forcing your mind, without any critical judgement of self, with your eyes closed, just allow any visuals to float before you. Just be with the visuals, engage with them deeply and flow with them.

- Observe and feel what spaces, emotions and thoughts are coming and going. Float with the tide of memories. Resist the urge to judge, and do not fear the flow.
- You can repeat the same experience again and again with words like 'war', 'revenge', 'mother', 'soulmate', 'abundance', 'healing', etc. All these generic words contain a universe within, and we souls have been around and in situations that these words evoke. You can also say these words in your mother tongue. Your higher consciousness holds the memories of all these experiences over lifetimes. Allow them to surface without any resistance and see what happens.

If any of these self-explorations throw up any trauma, gently disengage from it and open your eyes. Calm down and remember that this is a past life memory and you are safe now. However, if the trauma feels deep and lingers on, I strongly recommend that you get in touch with a good regression therapist and revisit the traumatic past life when a therapist is holding space for you. If something creates an emotional charge, please look into it, as it is an indication of something unhealed there.

People who meditate frequently can do the exercise mentioned above in their meditations too.

It is advisable to book a PLR session if you want to delve deep into the light and shadow of your soul's innumerable and myriad incarnations spanning the pathways illuminated by time.

> *'I know that there is a reason for everything. Perhaps at the moment that an event occurs we have neither the insiight or the foresight to comprehend the reason, but with time and patience it will come to light.'*
> —**Dr Brian Weiss**

Chapter 7

Shadow Work and the Shadow Self

'I like my shadow; it reminds me that I exist.'
—Mehmet Murat ildan

After the success of Scottish author Robert Louis Stevenson's Gothic novella *Strange Case of Dr Jekyll and Mr Hyde*, published in 1886, the words 'like Dr Jekyll and Mr Hyde' became an epithet for two-faced individuals in common parlance. To date, this phrase is used liberally for people who display outward signs of extreme goodness and suddenly extreme evil, or for people who have hugely inconsistent mood swings, from happy to violent, and other such wildly aberrant behaviours, swinging from one end of the scale to the other.

So, who are Jekyll and Hyde?

Briefly, for the ones who have not yet read Stevenson's novella—a London lawyer, Gabriel Utterson, investigates strange happenings between his old friend Dr Henry Jekyll and a murderous criminal named Edward Hyde.

Actually, they are the same person but are split entities. Dr Jekyll invented a potion that would separate his evil shadow self (Hyde) from the amiable Jekyll. Towards the end of the book, evil Hyde has become the more dominant personality, taking over the persona of Jekyll. Hyde does not want Jekyll to go back to his original, lighter self. In the end, the violent, out-of-control Hyde dies by suicide in Jekyll's laboratory, wearing Jekyll's clothes. He finally kills the persona of Jekyll by killing himself.

Through his novella, Stevenson highlighted the duality of human nature, the eternal fight between good versus evil, the conflict of a dual existence.

And now, coming to psychology and psychoanalysis, Carl Jung, the Swiss psychiatrist and psychoanalyst mentioned earlier, wrote about the concept of the 'shadow' as part of his analytical psychology. He extensively discussed the shadow in his various writings.

The shadow self, however, is not necessarily evil per se. Our shadow is all the rejected, hated, denied and unsavoury parts of us that we are perpetually kicking into that dark closet, so they never surface in the light. Our denials are shoved away to dank places that we do not wish to visit. Often, our shadow persona is so deeply out of sight that we might never even suspect anything till one day it flares up and shakes the very foundations of our being.

Here is what Jung says about the shadow: 'The shadow is an inferior component of the personality and is consequently repressed through intensive resistance.'[1]

The 'inferior component' probably means all the 'undeveloped' parts of our personality, all the uncomfortable aspects we disregard.

The shadow self can be very innocuous, subtle even, hard to catch on to quickly by oneself or by others. Let me give you one example, dear readers.

In my twenties and thirties, I hugely disliked people who banged on tables to make a strong point or raised their voice to subdue other dissenting voices. I felt they were bullies and refused to engage with these personality types. As luck would have it, these loud types would lurk around at social get-togethers, parties and picnics, and voice their loud opinions soon enough. As they say, 'You can run but you can't hide.' So I decided not to run but to look within myself to

---

[1] 'The shadow: What you do behind your own', Jungian Analysis, https://www.counselinginzurich.com/the-shadow-carl-jung/.

figure why this personality type got under my skin. Why am I so sensitive to their loudness?

Since many of my answers come to me in my deepest meditations, I meditated on this precise question. Lo and behold, the answer came in a thunderous, revelatory flash! It shook me, and I did not like the answer particularly, but I could not hide from the truth of that revelation.

The answer came strong and clear: 'You are that person you dislike.'

I was outraged by this, and it took me a while to get over it. But once I did, I understood the meaning of that divine message. I am that person indeed. I don't bang on the table or scream loudly or use expletives to drive home a point, but I am opinionated. I am entrenched in my beliefs, sanctimonious while dispersing advice, I know a few cosmic secrets others don't and I am oh-so smug about it. I think I do this with a veneer of sophistication and self-deprecating humour, but boy, do I have all kinds of opinions about 'things'. So when someone mirrored my shadow loudly, it irritated me no end, because deep down I myself must have been terribly unhappy with my opinionated self. But it eluded cognizance in my conscious mind, and only after the digging was I able to reach the root.

Honestly, this peekaboo into my shadow was very painful but ultimately life-changing. I worked on myself to rotate my neck 180 degrees as often as I could and be open to hearing about other possibilities beyond my own knowledge and opinions. I continue to work on this aspect of mine to date; it is no more relegated to the shadows—the light shines on it and, physically, my neck feels lighter.

You may wonder why we are highlighting the shadow self in a separate chapter. Haven't we already shone a light on the emotional anomalies of the mind? Well, the shadow self can be firmly suppressed because of deep self-loathing for it, so much so that our denial can shove it to the innermost recesses of our mind. The shadow self can deceive the self and consequently deceive others. With denial, it can create patterns of self-sabotage or inflated egos. As these parts aggravate us, we judge or want to punish others who show off these traits—like I did in the past. Hence, it needs a little more discussion.

'Don't fight your demons. Your demons are here to teach you lessons. Sit down with your demons and have a drink and a chat and learn their names and talk about the burns on their fingers and scratches on their ankles. Some of them are very nice.'

—**Charles Bukowski**

I love this quote by Bukowski, the prolific writer who brutally showcased the depravity of urban life in America. Sadly, however, it is even more difficult to recognize the positive aspects of the shadow self, hovering beyond the self-loathing.

Interestingly, mythologies worldwide have stories of shadow selves of gods and goddesses, kings and warriors. Hades, the god of the dead in Greek mythology, Yama Dev, the god of death in Hindu mythology, and Chhaya, the consort of Surya Dev whose name literally literally means 'shadow' in Sanskrit, are some examples.

In Greek mythology, the first god in existence was named Chaos, the primordial personification of disorder and chaos at the beginning of the universe. It is wonderful that the Greeks believed the universe was birthed through chaos. And Nyx, Chaos's offspring, born asexually, is the goddess of the night and shadows.

In Hindu mythology, Chhaya is the goddess of shadow and is the sun god Surya Dev's consort (the Markandeya Purana tells the story of Chhaya). When Sanjna, the much-loved first wife of Surya, could not take the immense heat emanating from the body and aura of her husband, she created Chhaya, her own shadow image, for some respite from the burning heat of Surya Dev. One of Chhaya's children is Saturn (Shani Dev), whose direct gaze can wreak havoc on gods and humans and who is the chief justice of the universe, the god of karma, who will extract all karmic dues from souls, ultimately showing them the path of dharma. Surya Dev and Chhaya's other children are Savarni Manu and Tapti, the river goddess.

Sanjna's children with Surya Dev are Yama, the god of death and justice, and his twin sister, Yami, the goddess of the holy river Yamuna, and Shraddhadeva Manu. Yama is also known as Dharmaraja, the one who weighs the good and evil deeds of souls and hands out their retributions accordingly. Of course, when Surya Dev found out that Chhaya was a shadow of Sanjna, he was furious, but that story is for another day.

Then there is Kaal Bhairava, the fierce aspect of Shiva, the mightiest god of the Hindu pantheon.

Bhairava is commonly associated with annihilation. Originating in ancient Hindu legends, the much-feared form of Bhairava is revered by Hindus, Jains and Buddhists alike, worshipped throughout India and Nepal. Kaal Bhairava's consort is Bhairavi, the powerful aspect of Parvati, or Kali. This avatar of Lord Shiva is predominantly worshipped by the Aghori sect, a monastic order of ascetic Shaivite sadhus.

There are several legends surrounding Bhairava, the dark and frightful avatar of Shiva. According to the most popular legend, which features in the Vidyeshwara Samhita of Shiva Mahapurana, there was once a debate between Brahma, Vishnu and Shiva. Vishnu asked Brahma who the supreme creator of the universe was. Brahma became a little egotistical, as he was always celebrated as the creator. Furthermore, he thought that since he too had five heads like Shiva, he could achieve anything that Shiva could. He then began to forge the work of Shiva and started interfering with Shiva's daily duties.

Shiva observed all this patiently for some time. Later, when he could take it no more, he removed a small nail from his finger and threw it in anger. This nail assumed the form of Kaal Bhairava. The manifestation headed straight for Brahma and chopped off one of his heads. Bhairava is always shown holding the skull of Brahma in his hands.

Bhairava's action completely subdued and humbled Brahma, destroying his ego and bestowing instant enlightenment upon him. He was deeply grateful to Bhairava and, prostrating before him, promised to work only for the benefit of the universe from then on.

A modified version of the original legend goes as follows. When Brahma insulted Shiva, the latter took the form of the angry Bhairava. He jumped out from Shiva's third eye and severed Brahma's head. Brahma's head then got stuck to Bhairava's left palm. This was Bhairava's punishment for severing the most sacred and learned Brahmin's head. In order to atone for the greatest sin of Brahmahatya, Bhairava took a vow to wander around as a naked beggar, with the skull as his begging bowl. He is finally liberated of his sin when he reaches the holy city of Varanasi. There is still a temple dedicated to Bhairava's worship in this city.

Bhairava is considered to be the ultimate form for attaining liberation. He is the one who grants the awareness of pure consciousness. He pulls us out from the abyss of purgatory to the fountainhead of celestial light. This is much like our souls, seeking light and leaving the darkness behind. When we muster the courage to take a really good look at our shadow self and not abandon it or hide it, we give ourselves the chance to repair the abnormalities with therapy and spiritual healing. When the veil lifts, we see the gifts this self brings to us. We learn to work with strengths and not the weaknesses of our shadow and integrate this wisdom back into our human self.

Shadow work

How would you feel if you experienced a lack of belonging to the self every day? How would you cope if you had to keep boxing with your shadow self? How would you feel if a tall, dark shadow towered over you, making you feel overwhelmed?

When a creative young woman, Shalini C (name changed on request), felt all of the above, she sought me out for help. Here is her story in her own words:

'I kept tossing and turning on Sabari's couch in her clinic, trying to find the right words to capture my thoughts on the emerging "shadow self". In the healing, reflective mirror, I saw a lot of pain and darkness. You see, I was unable to recognize the image in the mirror.

'It seemed dark and morbid, uneasy in its existence. But that's exactly what I was all those years, uneasy in my existence. All my life, I never understood who I really was. That mirror that day just threw back at me all those layers I was carrying on me. Sabari very patiently worked with me, clearing that heavy feeling I held within. My body too had curled inwards, which physically led to many problems. Every session I had with her, I could trace where the pain was held, and with much hard work, we were able to physically release that emotion.

'Working with one's shadow can be very exhausting. I believe we all come into this world with a spectrum full of possibilities. But life has its own plan to take us where it wants to. These possibilities never really go away; they can be ignored or suppressed. If they don't leave you, your shadow carries all these possibilities for you. It's more powerful than you think; unfortunately, while fearing it or judging it, we lose out on its power. Life builds so many layers for us that we don't know who we really are. To my good fortune, the intensive soul work I did with Sabari helped me understand who I really am. It helped me get in touch with my feminine side. I embraced many changes physically and emotionally. Colours seemed to enter my life, and I felt purified in a nice way.

'From where I stand today, I feel much brighter and lighter. I no longer identify with the girl in that mirror, that dark shadow. But I do want to emphasize what a gift it was to unravel those layers when I had the chance to.

'I remember being a little girl sitting in the back seat of the car, whimsically lost in the lyrics that the radio sang. This was something I looked forward to—my parents would often take me on these drives. I always tried to catch every emotion the songs conveyed, the songs I tried to smell. I could shut out the noise around me, stare at the streets and get lost in the world the music transported me to. I had this deep fascination with the words and how they moved. I think somewhere it helped me emote a lot of what I was trying to escape. It made me realize there was a vacuum where I could feel without fear. I had a favourite line in each song, which I would save to experience someday in my life. This music meant a lot to me; it gave me an alternative reality where it was just me, free to be anything I wanted to be.

'As time passed, I grew up and life went on. Those songs and long drives were nothing more than a distant memory. Then, one day, I had to face that mirror Sabari placed in front of me. You see, nothing is ever truly forgotten. All those pent-up emotions had found a resting home in me, and the baggage had become too heavy for me to carry. Unknown to me, the answer was right there—it always had been. I had to write! Everything, I felt, needed to hold words. Only then was I able to make sense of them; otherwise, it was all lost and hidden. You see, that's how I identified with emotions as a child, so to understand myself I had to write. The whirlpool of words started pouring through me. Honestly, I never knew I held them inside. All I had to do was feel, and my hands would type. So here's what I felt a few years ago—I would like to share it with you:

My shadows walk beside me
Sometimes on the left, sometimes on the right

I can see one, two, three, four of them
They are all a part of me but still not joint

My consciousness didn't know them
Never noticed their silent play

I can hardly remember dragging them
Oblivion to my darkness I can say

But then things turned slow in life
I had to look around and inside

Shadows just don't follow you
One day I woke up and realized

They are shades of you
You don't seem to know anymore

Just like your head and heart
Won't leave you till you're no more

If you bring them in awareness
They can be your secret allies

Gifts you garner through time
Knitted to your soul in hard ties

Today I write to tell you my side
The shadow supports my write

It guides my fingers as I type
Awaken and alive on my other side.'

From darkness to light

Mustafa Ahmed is a very successful physical trainer whom celebrities flock to for training. Built like a lion but with the heart of a puppy, Mustafa is as endearing as they come. No one knew what he fought every day—silently, painfully—till he decided to give me a peek into his shadow self.

Here is Mustafa's story in his own words:

'I was twelve when I saw him for the last time. Just walking out the room while no one bothered to ask where he was going. That was the last time I saw my father. And since that day, he was the one I hated the most.

'For twenty-five years of my life, I carried this hatred in my heart. This hatred for my father for what he did to my mother, me and my brother and sisters.

No, he was not a wifebeater. No, he didn't beat me or my siblings or molest or even stare at us ever. But he used us to con the world. And left us while he ran away like a coward.

'Did he love us? I somehow believe he did. Did he care? I do believe he did. So, I always wondered, what was it that made him use us as a shield to save himself or as props to con people? It's something that always left me clueless.

'I remember my father calling home for the last time and to his luck, I answered the phone. And the last thing I said to him was: "If you believe in God, only ask for one thing. That we never meet again. Because if we do, that will be the last day of your life."

'Twenty-five years later, I met Sabari, whom my wife insisted I go to. Why? So that we could fix me and figure out the complexity of my brain and why I function the way I do. I must confess, I never believed in therapy or therapists, let alone hypnotherapy. But there I was.

'I liked Sabari from the word go. Somehow, I felt comfortable talking to her. But more importantly, I felt comfortable telling her my truth. And by truth, I mean my dark side. Or what I believed was my dark side.

'In our first session, the funniest thing happened. I passed out while listening to her calm voice and remember waking up after what seemed like hours. Worried, not knowing what she had got out of me in confession, I asked, "How long was I out for?" She smiled and said, "Fifteen minutes. You were having a good sleep. Snoring, even. Take the next three days off and rest." We both burst out laughing. I knew I could trust her with everything from that moment on.

'Now bear with me as I try to elaborate on an experience that would go on to define what I would say was the second wave of my life.

'I lie down on this comfortable bed, relaxing as I listen to Sabari's soothing voice. And before I know it, I am at a point of calmness where I can't feel my body.

'I find myself at what seems like a party. I walk around, seeing all these people dressed neatly and classily. All of a sudden, I see a man dressed in black. Black slim-fit shirt. Black trousers. With shiny black shoes and short hair gelled up. Fair-looking, strong-built and confident. You can sense he's got the limelight and he's loving it. The attention and everyone's eyes on him. This man is sharp, likeable and street smart. He knows how to survive. He knows how to deceive. This man, while being extremely charming, can use emotions to his benefit. You can sense he has a dark side to him, but one can't help but be charmed by him.

'In the other corner of the same room is a man who's dressed all in white. A man with an innocent smile. A face that seems like he has been hurt but knows how to hide it. He's conscious of how he looks. He is not sure of his capabilities. He's desperately seeking attention. He wants to be liked. He wants to belong. He simply isn't sure of whether he's going to make it in life.

'As I see both these men in the same room and yet poles apart, I notice their eyes meeting each other's. I see them look at each other for what feels like an eternity but is perhaps only a few seconds. It's at this point that the man dressed in black smiles at the man dressed in white. A smile of assurance. A smile with a thumbs-up sign, saying, "Don't worry. I got you. I will take care of us. You just be you." To which the man in white smiles back. A smile of gratitude and hope, knowing he will be okay. He will be fine. I realized immediately both these men are me. I saw both of them and I saw myself in them. I saw my face on both these men.

'And as I am processing all this, I find myself in what feels like a place above the clouds, everything around me was white. And suddenly, I see my father. He looks exactly the same as when I last saw him. He hasn't aged. He is just there, staring at me. At this point, I almost wake up, shouting and screaming, holding on to Sabari's hand so hard. Sabari places her hand with a little force on my forehead and pushes me back down. I somehow go back to the same place. I see my father again. He isn't talking, but I can hear him.

'He says, "I am not bad. I am not evil. I never wanted to hurt you. I never wanted to hurt anyone. I don't want you to hate me. I don't want you to think all that's bad in you is because of me. I did love you. How could I not? You are my son."

'But I don't want to forgive him. I don't want to listen to him. All I know is this man is the reason for my mother's suffering. Years of sorrow. Me not having a normal childhood. Never being able to make friends. Always being a loner.

'As these thoughts are churning, I see the blurred face of a woman—a woman dressed in a white Afghan dress. I can't see her face, but somehow, I can sense her eyes locked on me. And again, she isn't saying anything but I can hear her. I can hear her say, "You hold this hatred for my son. You hold this grudge against him. You spent years despising him. Believing that all he did was use you and the family. But have you ever thought of his pain? Ever thought of what his life was like growing up? Was he loved by his father? Was he treated right by those he loved? What gives you the right to judge my son while you yourself know of your darkness? Darkness that you know is beyond your control or understanding. Darkness that you know, if they could see, would make the world question your sanity. And yet you judge him. Yet you hate him. While all that you hate about him is what has helped you survive. Let go of my son. Let me take him. Let him be at peace." I cry and howl. There are tears gushing down my cheeks. I can't let him go again. I will be lost. I can't.

'And again this woman says, "He's my son. My first-born. Imagine if you were taken away from your mother and were not let go of because of someone's hatred for you. What would you feel? Let my son go. He's not evil. He's not bad. He is you and you are him. Or, at least, a part of him."

'At this point, like a flash of lightning, something shifts in me and I can't hate him. I can't hold this anger against him. I see my father as just a man. Without any prejudice or judgement. Just a man who has struggled through life.

'I let go of my father as his mother, my grandmother, whom I have never met or seen, holds his hand and walks away into the clouds while I cry unstoppably. I see my father turn and smile. And again, he doesn't say anything, yet I hear him saying, "Thank you. I love you, son."

'I am slowly brought back to my senses by Sabari. The first thing I ask her is if she's okay. Even though I was not in my senses, I knew I had been holding her hand hard and must have scared her. But her reply left me smiling and astonished. She said, "Mustafa, I am Shiva's daughter. Nothing can hurt me."

'As I start to feel normal, we speak about what I saw in more detail. And for the first time, I realize that what I hated about my father, everything I thought that was wrong with and evil in him, was what helped me survive, what made me successful, what made me win in life. The charm, the tenacity and the will to succeed, even the smooth talking.

'I understood that the man dressed in black held all the traits of my father, while the one dressed in white was the core me. But I needed some of my father's traits not just to survive but also to be the best version of myself. It is what made me the best at what I did and achieve accolades.

'But most important of all, it made me accept my darkness and made me understand that I can use it. I don't have to let it control me—instead, I can control it for my own good. It made me understand that the man dressed in black kept his promise. He did take care of the man dressed in white. He made sure they were both okay.

'I can just say that I wish and pray for everyone to be able to accept their darkness, for it's the only way to achieve enlightenment.

'Love and only love for Sabari. I trust this woman with my life.'

Through the two accounts from Shalini and Mustafa, you read the free flow of their consciousness, which these souls have shared so bravely with the world. They struggled for years with their shadows, then decided to go head-on and 'look' at their shadow selves. Theirs was a huge battle, but they ultimately won the battle with compassion and healing. They honoured their shadow selves, and understood and integrated them beautifully and creatively to feel wholesome and desired.

We can all do the same and live in cognizance of the shadows in and around us. Shadow work needs to be done with a trained therapist and healer. It is difficult to process the intensity and subtlety of our shadows, so having a trained therapist hold space for us is advisable. As I always say, seek help and you will receive it.

Chapter 8
Life Between Lives Therapy

'We are divine but imperfect beings who exist in two worlds, material and spiritual. It is our destiny to shuttle back and forth between these universes through space and time while we learn to master ourselves and acquire knowledge.'
—Michael Newton

Our travels back home into the spirit world

When we reminisce about a deceased person, we tend to glance upwards towards the sky, like the person is residing somewhere amidst the clouds. When a small child innocently asks about a favourite pet who has passed away, or about anyone closely bonded to them who is no longer around, and we are unable to explain the finality of death to them, we might say, 'Your nana is now a star up there ...' or 'Biscuit is there, playing with his friends ...' as we point towards the heavens. And the little one, with complete love and faith, sends a flying kiss up heavenwards to the loved one.

Before starting to write this chapter, I was thinking about this phenomenon, which cuts across cultures, religions and mindscapes—where we look upwards towards the skies while wishing love and wellness to the soul of a person who is not physically present on the planet.

Who taught us this spontaneous action when acknowledging a deceased one? Or do our souls intrinsically know where we go after a physical incarnation a thousand times over? We mimic the actions of our elders, and when we are elders, our youngsters mimic our actions and this silent acknowledgement of a loved soul—living, breathing in the fluffy clouds in the skies—continues.

I was born curious, I think, and the mythical stories of gods and goddesses and their good and even naughty deeds was my oxygen. When my paternal and maternal grandmothers, excellent storytellers both, narrated these stories to keep the precocious child of a working mother engaged, they won hands down. My attention never wavered and, goggle-eyed, I lapped up these stories of worlds unbeknownst to me. Metaphorically, I was in heaven.

Even as an adult, I love reading stories from Greek and Roman mythology—in fact, mythologies from around the world. Riveting tales of gods and goddesses who mirrored the humans they wanted to control give insights into faults, fatalities, largesses and a wide spectrum of behavioural manifestations, and I find it all extremely fascinating.

I remember when I was around six years of age, I used to stand in front of the mirror with deep concentration, focusing on my face, my eyes, and I would keep asking myself—'Who is Sabari? Where is my home? Do I belong here? Where did my parents come from? Is this how I will look?' I would feel some kind of energetic thrumming in my body, like some forgotten melody trying to burst open. I felt I needed to remember, I had to, but I just could not—the memories eluded me. It was pretty weird, but I felt compelled to do this check in the mirror. Always, while looking into the mirror, I was trying to bore through the gaze of my eyes. And then suddenly, I would be so viscerally normal, enjoying and negotiating bends in the river, when required in my daily life.

As a child, I loved drawing with coloured pastels in my drawing book. My favourite pastime was to go up to the open terrace of my childhood home and draw, mostly before sunset, trying to capture the mesmerizing hues of the clouds, the pinks, the violets, the goldens and the oranges. I absolutely loved watching the clouds shift shape and colour. And as I looked at the clouds, I often wondered what was behind them. Who lived there? The abode of the gods and goddesses, right? Would they ever, just once, peek out and see me?

The adults in the house were content that I was drawing on the terrace because this meant they didn't have to watch over me. I never dared tell anyone my actual thoughts and feelings, about staring at the clouds and talking to the mirror. They just happened and then slowly ceased during my preteen years.

If you have experienced the above at any point in your life and hesitated to share it with anyone fearing judgement, relax. It is not abnormal to have churnings when one is getting used to being in Earth school and adjusting to a new body and a heavier energy frequency. Some souls adjust quickly, while others may take longer. I took a bit of adjustment to embrace humanhood; it's all good. But school is never home, however knowledge-filled or fun-filled the ride is, and hence, in some moments of weakness or great joy, we look up heavenwards to our real home, feeling deep within that soulmates and guides from back 'home' are watching over us.

Michael Newton, an American hypnotist and author, stumbled upon the information that we all have a loving home up there in the spirit world during one of his client sessions. His first book, *Journey of Souls*, was published in 1994. This book had a great impact on spiritual seekers, who read detailed descriptions of the spirit world, soulmates, soul groups, spirit guides and life and body choices through the first-person accounts of Newton's patients, who, under deep hypnosis, could connect with this spiritual realm and relay the information back.

An atheist by admission, Newton threw himself into researching this spiritual regression to 'home', rigorously and relentlessly, often doing three to four sessions a day. A typical LBL session can last four to five hours, so you can imagine how many hours of uncompromising work he was putting in. He recorded incredible accounts of thousands of clients about their lives after death and their preparations to come into their current lives. Newton listened to descriptions of various soul relationships, which we also bring forward in our various incarnations in Earth school. These weren't scraps of information but solid accounts of souls who have been there, done that. In this mammoth task of collating all this gob-smacking information, Michael was ably and lovingly supported by his wife, Peggy Newton. Peggy was a quiet force by herself and held everything together with her innate wisdom and intelligence—she was the wind beneath Michael's wings. And fly he did, when his second book, *Destiny of Souls*, was published in the year 2000 and he came to be regarded as a global authority on afterlife research.

I first read *Journey of Souls* in 2009, quickly followed by *Destiny of Souls*. I was so tuned into *Journey of Souls* from the word go that I felt a sense of deep comfort and relief—a comfort and relief in 'knowing'

I truly belong somewhere, in my eternal home. My conversations with myself in front of the mirror from so long ago, my trying to peer through clouds—all over again, it made effortless sense. Of course, the forgotten melodies will want to thrum through me because they are never actually forgotten. Every cell memory flows with my soul song of eternal being.

I was a newbie, a practising regression therapist, but I was sure that I wanted to learn LBL therapy, which felt so spiritually right for me when I read and reread Michael Newton's books.

My dream came true, and I was able to enroll in one of the trainings at the Michael Newton Institute in the UK, conducted in the summer of 2012. Experiencing my own LBL session, and the training itself was nothing short of life-changing. I met beautiful spiritual co-travellers, excellent teachers and mentors, and, at the end of it, my heart was exploding with love.

A very interesting incident happened during my training. Right after the orientation, we were asked to choose a partner with whom we would share intensive spiritual work for the next few days, through the course of our training. Students looked around, smiling tentatively, taking stock of who could be their partner through this very significant time of learning. I decided not to move, knowing my partner would find me. Before I could breathe this thought out into the universe, I felt a light tap on my shoulder. I turned around to see the smiling face of

Allison Lee Axinn, a vibrant mentor shepherding our motley group. Allison said, 'Would you like Franklin to be your partner?'

I shifted my gaze to a smiling six-foot-plus white man with twinkling blue eyes and neatly combed silver hair. He was handsome and had a casual charm about him. He smiled, extending his hand out. 'Franklin Sluitjers.' I said, 'Why not? Hello, Franklin.' He engulfed my extended palm in his long-fingered hand, and I immediately felt at ease. I liked his long fingers and later discovered he is a fine pianist when he played the piano at our rocking wrap party, the mellifluous notes echoing around the country-house-turned-hotel in which we were staying. Franklin was a doctor, a practising medic in the Netherlands, interested in many holistic therapies besides modern medicine.

Our intensive and extremely interesting training started, and as it unfolded and we went through experiential exercises, Michael's books started to come alive, as we were living and breathing his processes. Finally, the day arrived when we were to work with our partners to facilitate individual sessions while being watched over by our mentors. This was the holy rite of passage, which, if we passed, would certify us and allow us to practise LBL therapy.

I was in a state of nervous excitement but also calm within, focusing on the workshop training manual and the processes so that Franklin, my partner, could have a great LBL session. The mentor for our team was Pernille Lund, a vivacious Danish healer who is very wise, yet carries her wisdom in a light and jovial way. I am indebted to Pernille in multiple ways. When I was confused and needed deeper understanding when my kidneys were failing, I reached out to Pernille and, in just one long session with her, she opened my psychic eyes to the reason of this dis-balance in my body. Armed with the blazing penny drop, which Pernille facilitated for me in our session, I coped so much better with my journey forward with this vital malfunction in my physical body.

Back to the day of our one-on-one student facilitations at the Newton Institute LBL training. The day arrived bright and shining, and I remember I could smell the aroma of freshly mowed grass. Watched over by Pernille, I facilitated Franklin's session as a therapist. Pernille passed me notes when she thought I could dig deeper in certain places. I took her guidance and overall, I must say, the session went quite well. Franklin received some invaluable insights and was quite happy. I too was happy that I did well.

Buoyant, we went down to lunch, the big dining hall bustling with excited students who had all just experienced their first LBL session, role playing as client and therapist. After lunch, the roles would be reversed, and the client would become the therapist.

I hardly ate, keeping all my channels lighter, not wanting to feel heavy with a full stomach. Once we were back in the room, I lay down on the bed, the warm sun pouring its golden hues into the room through the window, which faced a beautiful garden. Franklin sat in the therapist's chair, his recorder and notebook ready.

What can I say? I had an incredible session where I went back home, to where I belong, my soul soaring up in joy, receiving sacred knowledge and making deeper sense of things as a mortal who was now connected to her highest soul connection and being allowed, being blessed, to receive so much from the divine, which gave direction to my mortal life. Oh, what a wonderful play between the conscious, the subconscious and the superconscious minds. I have had PLRs before, through which I learnt a lot about my soul journey, and transformations took place within, but this was on a different level.

Michael Newton was so right when he said, 'In my view, the difference between past life regression and spiritual regression is that LBL therapy allows for an easier transformation of perception.' And now, after years of being an LBL therapist, I know for a fact that this is true. Soul memories of our eternal home are stored in the superconscious mind, and accessing that during an LBL session is an altogether different experience. It's the highest spiritual connection one can make with their soul mind while still in a physical body.

I felt a silence within me after the session. With half-closed eyes, I just beamed for a while. Then, finally, I sat up and registered the radiant faces of Franklin and Pernille. They knew how deeply meaningful the just-concluded LBL session had been for me.

Still excited, I requested Franklin to play back a bit of the session recording. He rewound a little and pressed the play button. What came out of the recorder was 'zzzzzzzz'! He looked at the recorder quizzically, rewound some more and pressed play again—'zzzzzzzzzzzzzzz'. Alarmed, I asked Franklin to check if the recorder had recorded the session at all. He showed me the timeline on the recorder: three-plus hours of data had been recorded. But every time we tried to play the data, all it offered was a crackling 'zzzzz'.

Needless to say, I felt crushed by this huge disappointment. My first LBL, my precious LBL, never would I hear it again. Obviously, I did not even attempt to hide my disappointment, a hint of anger too, and everyone rallied around me to make me feel better about this colossal loss. I did not feel better but decided to step back from it, as there was a debrief scheduled and the day's curriculum was not over.

That night, when the quietness was highlighted by intermittent creaks and groans coming from the old country house, I sat down to meditate. Nearly all my answers are found in a deep meditative state, when I am able to cut out the extraneous noise. I meditated on why I could not hear my session recording when every other student could hear theirs.

Through layers of consciousness and stillness, the answer floated up like a tiny beacon of light. A voice told me, 'We thought it would be better for you not to hear this recording.' My mind in a tizzy, free-falling, I asked, 'Who decided this? And why?'

Suddenly, I could feel the presence of one of my closest spiritual guides, Meher Baba. He said, 'All who guide and help you thought this is better because we do not want you to have even the smallest sense of artificial pride and ego, because going forward, you will be doing the critical work of healing and helping people.'

I fell silent in shock. Meher Baba continued with extreme kindness, 'Of course, you will remember everything that you received from us today, and your life will be enhanced with this guidance and knowledge, but no other person needs to know or hear about your sacred experience.'

Slowly but surely, I got the drift. I had experienced myself as a teacher in the spirit world who works with very young souls, souls who are preparing for their earliest incarnations. I teach them fearlessness so they can choose action-oriented, meaningful lives and grow spiritually, beyond fear and weakness. Incidentally, a huge number of my clients come to me to get over fears of various kinds so that they can claim their lives back and walk the life path they are meant to walk on.

I felt a sudden chill and a bit sad that in my human avatar I need saving from the vice-like grip of arrogance and ego, so easy to fall prey to. Up there, there is no ego, as there is no separation between soul, body and mind. I felt the deepest gratitude again for my guides and kindred souls, who are with me on my journey and are silently taking care of the pitfalls along the way so that I don't fall but rise to my highest potential. From that moment on, all my disappointment, anger and frustration at not having a recording of my first LBL experience just vanished into that summer night. Poof! The divine beings freed me again. I decided that whatever work I have ordained for myself while creating the blueprint of this life is the most important thing. I need to fulfil that with honesty and empathy. And I do have an elephantine memory, so, thankfully, nothing will be forgotten; the conversations and feelings that came up during my session are locked in every layer of my consciousness.

I have undergone the teacher training in LBL in America, and have taught and facilitated a training workshop in Australia. I have set up many group meetings for spiritual seekers in India, talking about the afterlife, and I have facilitated countless LBL sessions in my peaceful clinic.

Typically, in an LBL session, we begin with a deep induction, helping the client connect with the superconscious mind. We move on to some memory warmups, asking the client, under deep hypnosis, to relive a few happy or neutral childhood memories. We then facilitate the client in remembering the soul memories of when they were in the womb. The womb is a very important place because that's the first time the client experiences the soul self. The womb throws up vital information about life and body choices; hence, it is a goldmine of a stop. Then we take the client back to the immediate past life before they incarnated in this life. We explore the past life briefly, leading to the physical death and then the journey to the spirit world. Every stop in the session is important, but the journey of the soul to the spirit world is where the definitive LBL experience begins.

Going back home

Now let us deep dive into what really happens during an LBL session. Below is a recounting of the session of my dear friend and colleague, Aman, a gentle healer with tremendous inner strength, which he emanates into his clients. We have done multiple healing sessions with each other over the years, which have always helped lighten our emotional loads. In fact, Aman is the one who introduced me to Michael Newton's work and urged me to read *Journey of Souls*. For this nudge and for many other things, I shall remain eternally grateful to him. So it was only natural that when I came back to India after my LBL training, I offered to facilitate a session for Aman. This is one of my earliest LBL sessions, and I am including this here because it gives a wealth of information about our spirit world, and because I was just freshly minted as an LBL therapist at the time, with my heart fluttering in my rib cage, so it is a raw and fresh take.

After a nice induction and some memory warmups of his childhood memories, Aman's soul floated into the womb. He said, 'It is dark ... but I am comfortable. I can sense my mother's heartbeat.' Allowing himself to go deeper into the experience, Aman sensed that his mother was at her own mother's house, surrounded by Aman's aunts, and they were all having a good time.

When I asked Aman how his soul was feeling in the womb, he said he was feeling excited and a little scared. He went on to say that the purpose of his life as Aman was to teach others how to love.

I asked, 'Do you feel ready ...?'

Aman said, very calmly, 'The time has come. Though there is a little reluctance ...'

I asked him, 'What kind of reluctance? Feel deeper into it.'

He took a longish pause. It is imperative that the therapists give extra processing time to the client in the womb, as this is the first time the client is accessing soul memories and experiencing their self as a soul without a firmed-up physical body, floating in amniotic fluid.

Aman said, 'I have also chosen to allow myself to get intimidated. Especially when I am young ... till I learn.'

We spent some more time in the womb, where Aman told me that his chosen body and brain were a good match for the life he would live as Aman.

Then it was time to leave the womb and start our journey further back to his most immediate past life. We encourage and facilitate the client to access their most immediate past life before this current incarnation, as after physical death in the most immediate past life, the client's soul went home once again to make the blueprint for this life. Hence, that entry point back home is important.

Aman went back to a past life in which he was an English lady with an old-fashioned curly hairstyle, wearing a hat and a flowery dress, while standing on grass.

I used a deepening technique to focus his awareness further in his meditative trance and asked him to engage with his five senses, everything he was feeling, seeing, experiencing. He said he was feeling the presence of a man. He was wearing a suit. They were young and either married or 'together'. Aman said his past life persona was twenty-four years old and that that day they were hanging around outside as 'it's a day off'.

Aman moved forward in the timeline of that life. His name in that lifetime was Vivian. Vivian said the man was at the doorstep of his house and was asking her to run away with him. Vivian told the man she could not run away, and the man felt sad and distraught.

Vivian said, 'Eventually, the man died of a broken heart. I feel guilty, but I wasn't happy with him.'

We moved on and Vivian was now with a partner who gave her a great sense of comfort. Vivian said the year was either 1910 or 1920.

Vivian further elaborated that she felt deeply pained that she had caused so much distress to another human and had caused a death from a broken heart. Vivian felt she was carrying this cross.

I moved Vivian to the last day of her life.

Aman said, 'I am sitting on an armchair. I am in my seventies.'

To gentle questions, Vivian said her partner (Aman's current wife Uma) had already gone to the spirit world. She felt the presence of the current life daughter, who was also the daughter in Vivian's lifetime.

Vivian's death was peaceful. She said, 'It's about time ...' Her only regret was that she had caused emotional pain to someone who had loved her.

Her soul mind did not hang around after her physical death, and quite immediately, her soul started floating up.

Souls are different. After physical death, some souls stay around to process things and say goodbyes, and must gently be guided up into the spirit world. Our dear old soul Aman needed no such encouragement, and off he went where he needed to go.

Vivian kept floating up to the realm of an all-knowing spiritual power, her soul feeling the joy of being released from the fetters of the physical body.

After a longish silence, Aman said that a vortex of purplish-white was 'descending' on him, surrounding him. A sense of waiting prevailed over him.

During this stage, when the client is at the gateway of the spirit world, adjusting on a soul level to everything around them, the therapist needs to encourage the client gently, but never push for hasty answers, and needs to allow the client to process the experience at their own pace. However, we can never allow the silence to be too long, or the connection with the client may be broken. Focusing and deepening the client through the LBL session is wise and an absolute requirement.

I asked Aman, 'Is your personal spirit guide around?'

Visibly, Aman was trying to figure something out.

He said, 'I sense a short, stocky male wearing armour, and with him a tall figure with flowing white hair and a long white beard, a very warm, benign presence. They are so different from each other ...'

I asked him to focus deeper by saying, 'Go closer ... Feel their energies. Who is your personal spirit guide?'

Aman replied, 'The one with the long hair. The shorter guy is here to clear the way, he says.'

I asked, 'Check if you have permission to know your guide's name.'

Aman replied, 'Aza.'

I said, 'Ask your guide—does he have a message for you?'

Aman said, 'This is not the final place. He has come to take me … I have to go somewhere.'

Guided by his spirit guide, Vivian/Aman's soul mind moved deeper into the spirit world. Long silences are natural when the soul experiences this journey through the superconscious mind. Gentle nudges and soft, non-leading questions are welcome to make the memories come up clearly.

Aman said, 'A lot seems to be happening.'

He said he was floating through a dark space and that Aza was with him. I guided him into a deeper trance. I asked him to continue the journey and be aware of his surroundings and feelings.

Aman said, 'It feels like I have come out of a dark cave. I am outdoors in a very beautiful and scenic place. I am standing at the edge of a water body. I don't see Aza but I know he is there.'

I said, 'Connect with your soul mind and ask Aza—how did you do in your life as Vivian?'

Aman said, 'I made the right choice. And I needn't carry the guilt.'

In his expanded state of consciousness, Aman travelled with Aza to meet his soul group. He sensed himself floating towards a cluster of individual orbs of light. I urged him to go closer and closer towards the cluster.

As he went closer, he saw the cluster appearing like a big star. The star spread out in a semicircle around him, and Aman said he was in the centre of the semicircle. I immediately knew that he was amid his soul group.

A soul group is composed of souls with the same energy signatures working towards a common goal. The souls often incarnate together through their various lifetimes, helping each other learn lessons and grow, both through good and bad experiences.

In his book *Destiny of Souls*, Michael Newton wrote that homecoming is a joyful interlude, particularly after a life with little karmic contact between a soul and its soulmates. Michael Newton's hypnosis subjects have said they were greeted with embraces, joy and laughter.

A cluster group typically consists of fifteen souls but can be bigger or smaller. The soul's growth determines how subjects perceive their group cluster environment, although schoolroom recollections are usually quite distinct. A cluster group consists of souls with similar levels of spiritual growth, each with its own strengths and weaknesses. This mix balances the group.

The soul group

Aman saw a bright light coming forward to greet him. He said it was Uma, his wife in this current lifetime. Remember, a part of our soul energy is always intact in the spirit world and never incarnates. So here was Uma meeting Aman in their pristine soul selves.

Aman said, in a voice choked with emotion, 'She is holding me tight.'

Tears of joy were pouring down his cheeks. I kept quiet and gave him time to feel this ethereal love while still in the physical body. Then Aman said that Uma was his primary soulmate and that they had incarnated together over multiple lifetimes but had had many partings, though they 'will always be together'. Aman still sounded very emotional and overwhelmed while telling me all this.

I guided Aman to focus deeper and asked him, 'What is your eternal soul name?' We are all different energies in the spirit world, with different names. In every LBL session, the client finds out their soul names. Sometimes it's a sound, sometimes a letter of the alphabet, sometimes a proper name. Don't ask me how we get our soul names—I do not know, but we do have names. I found out my soul name during my first LBL session, facilitated by Franklin. My soul name is Azzara.

Aman spelt out his soul name: R-O-Z-. Roz was his name.

When I asked him to tell me the soul name of his primary soulmate, after some deep concentration, Aman said, 'Aahs or Ash … something like that. I am not fully sure.' Then, after a while, Aman said, 'She is teasing me and telling me that in another lifetime, she will choose her name to match my spirit name, Roz.'

And we thought our parents named us! Since Aman seemed pretty pleased with that information, who was I to dissent?

The best part of our session was when Roz saw me in his soul group. I was happy but not surprised, because we have close bonds over lifetimes. Roz was a little surprised and found it funny. As Aman, he was smiling. He said the colour around me was golden. When I asked, 'What is the soul contract between us?', he said, 'Spiritual growth.'

Let me share a funny incident that happened when I was facilitating a past life session for Aman. In that life, he was a Greek philosopher and teacher. At the death scene, when I asked who was around, Aman said that I was sitting next to him (him, in that life) and holding his hand. He said that I was a fellow Greek philosopher at the Lyceum. Quite overwhelmed, I asked what my name was in that life, and he said, 'Aristotle.'

I had to take some quick deep breaths to stabilize myself. Aristotle? Philosopher, linguist, polymath … influenced by Plato and Socrates … that Aristotle? My heart was thumping with excitement, but with an effort of will, I kept my voice calm because I had to steer the session to its healing resolution.

As soon as Aman integrated, opened his eyes and looked at me, I said, 'Aman! I was Aristotle! The Aristotle! Wow!'

Smiling, Aman said in a calm voice, 'Oh no. Aristotle was a common name at that time in Greece.' Poof! Was that the sound of my ego deflating? We both had a good laugh about it.

Coming back to our LBL session—after the soul group, Aman went with Aza to a place that looked like a library, filled with books. Aman said his Akashic records were there.

Being a healer/therapist, Aman obviously knew about the Akashic records, which are the records of every soul since its inception. They are the records of the past, present and future, with the past– present– future happening in the now. At this juncture, we will not be discussing quantum physics, but suffice it to say, hundreds of Michael's clients have gone to a library space in the spirit world and received guidance from their book of life (these case studies are from *Journey of Souls*).

A visit to the library

Without any hesitation, Aman was guided to go towards a thick book, which he felt had his soul name and current life name written on it. I asked him to pick up the book and ask his soul mind what he was supposed to understand from this book.

Aman said unhesitatingly, 'Patterns ...'

Aman opened the book, and the first page had the Kenyan flag on it.

I tuned him in deeper to understand the information that the divine beings were allowing him to access at that moment. Interestingly, Kenya had a special place in Aman's life. He had lived there for a few years and loved it, but had to come back to India due to personal reasons. His soul longed to go back and live in Kenya; however, the required connections were not happening.

Aman said, 'My masters have chosen me to go to Kenya. I have to do some work ... spread something.'

Aza, Aman's spirit guide, was a celestial presence in the background at that moment. I asked Aman to check with Aza and his masters why he had to go to Kenya. After a long silence, he said, 'It's a challenge for every aspect of my soul's growth. And it's a choice. It would be good if I made that choice.'

I asked, 'If it is a challenge, which part challenges Roz?'

Aman replied, 'To break free and become independent.'

I said, 'Unlike the life you came from? Vivian's life, carrying the guilt? Is Vivian's life an important incarnation for your soul's growth?'

Aman replied, 'Hmm. In terms of the pattern ...'

I then asked him to delve deeper into his Akashic records to see if Roz had any other soul patterns he needed to look into or any guidance about what his soul was really good at and had mastered over lifetimes.

Aman said, 'Anger is coming.'

We went deeper into the anger and why it was required, but Aman told me he was breaking that pattern now.

I asked him, 'What else is your book showing?'

Aman replied, 'It keeps jumping ... pictures. I am shown pages of energy work ... I have done a lot of healing work ...'

I asked him, 'You have been a healer many times?'

Aman quickly said that he was drawn to ancient healing practices, like Tibetan, Chinese and Reiki healing. Then he added in a mysterious voice, 'I have to make other people aware ... of that, I am aware. Especially help people who are stepping into a better life, a better understanding. I have to be the bridge.'

I was very intrigued by Aman's words and guided him deeper.

I asked him, 'What work do you do in the spirit world?'

Yes, we all do jobs upstairs. Jobs that suit our soul signatures and eternal temperaments.

Aman replied after a long silence, 'I do some healing with my hands. Uma (his current life wife), also does this kind of work ... We work together.'

I asked, 'So you are a healer?'

Aman said, 'Something about babies …'

I asked him, 'What babies? What is it that you do?'

Aman replied after a beat, 'Nurture baby souls.'

I asked, 'Do you get them ready for something?'

Aman replied, 'I work with souls that died young in their incarnations. As babies … When they come back, I heal them. I love them. I teach them also.'

There is so much discussion in healer communities about sudden infant death syndrome. It is also said that a soul chooses a life, but when it actually incarnates in that chosen life and realizes that the conditions are not right for soul growth, it can choose to come back to the spirit world. It may try again later, or maybe not. Was Aman privy to that knowledge? I was excited.

Aman said, 'I am just seeing myself at work.'

I asked him, 'What are you doing? What do you look like? Male, female, androgynous?'

Aman replied, 'I look female and very delicate … soft-looking.'

Aman now had to put away his book of life, as he was told that he was not allowed to see the last few pages.

After some more time in the library, it was finally time to move on.

I asked Aman if it was time to go meet the elders, the wise beings who always guide us through our various incarnations. After a short silence, Aman said, 'Yes, but after a short detour.' He had to go to the place where all the animal souls were.

The animal kingdom

Aman said excitedly, 'Oh, I know them. I know some of the doggies. It's an outdoor area with a big garden. There is an indoor area as well. I have many bonds with these dogs.'

I asked him, 'Do you have bonds with them over lifetimes?'

Aman replied, 'I have worked with many of these animals.'

I gave him some time to feel this animal space, where he felt so connected, having worked with and loved many of these animal souls.

For all of you who have loved and lost your beloved pets and wondered what is beyond that rainbow bridge, you can rest assured knowing there is a beautiful space of care and love in the spirit world for all animal souls. Also, fragments of a beloved pet's energy never leave us; they hover around, enveloping us in love and looking after us.

Once, in New Orleans, Indranil and I were staying in a beautiful old house in Faubourg Marigny, and I took some pictures with the owners in their living room. When I looked at the pictures, I saw multiple tiny orbs shining in the frame. I was curious because it was flat light in the room, so where did the orbs come from?

And then I remembered. I had asked the owners if they had always had pets over the years. They said yes, they had had multiple cats over the years. I immediately recalled seeing two cats in the house during this visit. I showed them the pictures and pointed out the orbs. I said that the soul fragments of their departed cats, their companions, were still hovering around them. They felt the same, interestingly, and said they could pick up the energies of their cats around them.

The council of wise beings

Accompanied by Aza, his primary spirit guide, Aman finally went to meet the council of elders (as Michael called them)—the wise beings.

With his inner hearing, he heard them discussing his current life as Aman, and they concurred that he was doing pretty well.

Aman said, 'I have done well, especially from the child I chose to be, and now it's reaching its pinnacle. The growth ...'

Some of the life lessons and issues Aman's soul had chosen to work with had now reached their pinnacle, and he was meant to understand this. Hence, directions were being given to him through that LBL session.

As a therapist, again and again I have observed that the universe gives permission for an LBL session when a soul is at a crossroads of some kind. The reading up on, the interest and the finding of a therapist happens organically when the knowledge is meant to be received. When the time is right, the session happens.

In fact my session with Aman was cancelled three times, because of one reason or the other, and eventually happened, without our realizing it, at 12.12 on 12.12.12 ! Talk about perfect timing.

The wise beings told Aman that, going forward, he had to follow his intuition more than ever. They said, 'Don't hold back ... Seize all opportunities.'

I asked him, 'What is the most important lesson you have chosen to learn in this lifetime?'

Aman said, 'Breaking free from the expectations of others.'

What followed thereafter was a masterclass in spiritual guidance—a session filled with constructive criticism from the wise beings and a treasure house of wisdom that would light the path in front of him, nudge him to make the right choices and fuel the required actions for his growth.

In this precious meeting with the council of wise beings, Roz's soul had many, many questions. All his whys were answered by the wise beings, who communicated to him, 'Do not worry. Everything in our current life has been planned right down to the last detail.'

After the meeting, Aman was very clear that he wanted to go back once more to his soul group to understand more about a close soul member. Some enlightening, expansive soul understanding followed, and it was clear that Aman indeed had to come back to his soul group. These were very private conversations, so I shall not write them here, but it's always amazing how the soul knows with an inner knowing and does not hesitate to follow guidance.

After nearly three hours, I could feel that it was time for the session to wind down and for Aman to come back and integrate back into his current life.

Aza said that he would be sending the right people to aid him in his life's work. That felt wonderfully comforting to Aman.

I asked him, 'How are you feeling now that you are about to leave your spirit home?'

Aman replied, 'Very light, very comforted, knowing that all these earthly things are just ... games.'

I brought Aman back and integrated him fully into his body and current consciousness. This is a very important part of any session, as experiencing an LBL session is quite like an out-of-body experience.

Chatting after the session, I asked Aman, 'Now how do you understand yourself better with all the spiritual knowing you felt and received?'

Aman replied, 'The relationships. I understand them better now.'

I asked him, 'Do you now have a better comprehension of life and your place in it?'

Aman replied after a pause, 'I feel that everything in my life is as it should be.'

I said, 'Isn't that wonderful?'

Aman replied, 'Yes, and no more sweating about it. This morning, I picked up an angel oracle card from the pack before coming here. The card I picked with my eyes closed was Divine Order—everything as it should be.'

Divine order it is for us all. I couldn't stop smiling. I felt so happy for my friend. Precious times, precious learnings. I have to concur that the universe is truly held together by a divine order.

Spiritual wisdom twice over

Below are the LBL reflections of a bright and successful businesswoman. This is her account in her own words:

'I had approached Sabari for PLR to help me understand and cover distance in resolving dimensions of love that were bothering me. After some sessions, Sabari proposed that I explore LBL. I had developed a trusted bond with her by then and agreed to explore. The first LBL was a beautiful experience, and I experienced this feeling of being in a new place where different energies and people were holding me, giving me words of wisdom, taking me around. Towards the end, I also received two clear messages that set me thinking deeply later.

'Wanting to do a second LBL was intuitive, and I had this realization somewhere that there was a message that I needed to hear. I spoke to Sabari and asked if she felt we could do a second session. She was measured in her agreement but was excited. She did, however, mention that she does a second LBL generally following a calling and does not normally propose it herself.

'The second LBL session was very different from the first one. It was a session where we exchanged messages with my guides that were fundamental to how I was living my life. It was as if someone was trying to give me a glimpse of deeper dimensions.

'After a journey of many difficult years, fighting my way through a difficult life, it seemed like someone brought me to this space of restfulness to give me a message that things were fine and would remain fine. There was also a message that the constant feeling of inadequacy was more a set of mental models and blocks rather than baggage from a previous life. I also felt like someone expanded my vision of help, which I could access whenever I felt overwhelmed. It seemed like this new place was not available just in that moment but that I could go back to these wise souls and access the wisdom later as well.

'The second LBL was profound and deep, and gave me a sense of a restful space where wisdom and comfort were available, which I experienced deeply during the session. It felt like something deep within me was integrated through visiting this space, and I connected with a part of me.'

Incredible shifts happen after an LBL session, and the feeling of liberation from doubts and old patterns is unimaginable, like wind beneath one's wings.

I would urge all of you to have an LBL experience at least once in your lives. When you feel from within the desire to have an LBL, listen to that voice with kindness. Plan it carefully by first choosing the right therapist, one who is well-trained to facilitate an LBL session. During first contact with your chosen therapist, just feel with your gut if they are the right one for you. There should be no compromises here.

If you don't meditate regularly, start a routine of meditation so that you can loosen your grip on your conscious mind and surrender easily to the higher, enlightened subconscious mind. Think and write down all the questions that you are seeking answers to in advance, and give them to your therapist. And above all, honour yourself and the process without any judgement or preconceived notions.

'When you die, you will be forced to lose everything, yet something will remain. It is the soul, which is real. Therefore, you should celebrate loss. The trappings of existence can fall away at any time; the essence will always remain. And that essence is you.'
— Dr Deepak Chopra, *Life After Death: A Burden of Proof*

Chapter 9

Assimilating All the Concepts, Therapeutic Modes and Healing

'The wound is the place where the Light enters you.'

—Rumi

In pain, in vulnerability, in brokenness, in worthlessness, we look around desperately for a ray of light. Thrashing around in the darkness of the mind, our souls seek healing and redemption. The wonderful thing is this is available in us and around us. Even if we reach out, hesitant, tentative and iffy, towards the healing light, the energy pulls us into the vortex of mending. We just need to be open to connect with our higher self, that pristine part of us that never incarnates and does not feel the blows and hits of human and other incarnations. Once we can align with the voice of our higher self, our core self, healing anything is in the realm of possibility. The only thing we need to do is open our mouths and ask for help. You will be surprised how the universe sends help in different ways, pronto. So my heartfelt advice is this: in suffering, just ask for help and it will come, quietly or with bells and whistles, but come it will.

As you hold this book in your hands and read these lines, know that we are connected through our heart chakras. I have written this book with love and brought to you the voices of my clients in their own words. I hope that you find some strength and courage in their stories of emotional freedom and choose to fill your own lives with love and healing.

Celebrated author and friend Namita Devidayal shares below how important it is to break free—from the emotional and mental chains that hold back the human experience in totality.

'It is so wonderful to have people like Sabari doing the work they do—helping us dive deep into parts of ourselves that we otherwise ignore or deflect or repress. I went to Sabari at a time when my rational mind had ceased to give me the answers I was looking for, and she guided me and prompted me to go into a place of nature where I could start decluttering the debris. It was an important moment that got me reflecting and started my journey inwards, which is arguably the most important journey in one's life.

'I hope, whether or not one has an "issue", that more people fearlessly explore their inner worlds—their fears, biases, dark and light selves—because that will lead to harmonious, peaceful living.'

Namita has written a book on her own healing journey and has had her own profound transformations on the path.

Indeed, the journey of self-discovery is the most compelling and satisfying journey a being can ever undertake, helping us find new horizons beyond the limiting perimeter of our human selves. Eventually, after all journeys, we find ourselves making that nostalgic journey back home—to the *me* within.

Spread your wings and fly

After recovering from a huge emotional setback, my client Vinda Tipnis now encourages everyone to jump into the pool of healing with trust and come out rejuvenated.

'It is often found that when women or men talk about their mental health issues with family or friends, they are met with common responses like: "Don't worry. Don't act like a weak person. It's overthinking; you are strong enough to deal with it all by yourself."

'These responses are because of a lack of knowledge regarding mental health issues, so please don't hesitate to seek help from a professional. God sent me an angel to help me. She is Sabari ... a sweet and very kind woman. I visited her for only four or five sessions and I was back to normal. So please reach out as soon as possible when you are suffering.'

You are the most important person in your life. Not in a selfish, self-absorbed way, but in a responsible, loving way. Once we learn to truly love ourselves, more and more love comes pouring into our lives. Love attracts love and hate attracts hate. This simple sentence holds an infinite, timeless lesson in it. Try living with love and feel what comes your way. Try living in hate and see what comes your way.

Ancient Hindu treatises like the Vedas and Upanishads offer a treasure chest of astute knowledge. This Vedic knowledge can be a beacon of light that has the power to illuminate our minds and help us make better sense of the business of living, both physically and metaphysically. Hinduism is more like a way of life, the goal of which is spiritual liberation and enlightenment—or moksha. Moksha means release from the eternal cycles of birth, death and rebirth. Every action of a good Hindu is geared towards achieving moksha.

However, in general terms, moksha is enlightenment of the mind. When one breaks free from cycles of negative patterns and allows the light to filter in, one receives the gift of enlightenment—the awakening of the authentic self.

The authentic self is somewhere deep within us, pure and untouched by external fires and independent of outer turmoil and change. Once you meet your true self, it will feel like a warm golden flame within, illuminating and giving you hope in the worst of times.

I have met and chatted with men and women who do good for their brethren in different ways. Some offer their physical presence, some donate to causes and some heal with their expertise. Many of these good people put others before them and forget to look after themselves in this whole business of caring. They forget they are mortals in physical bodies, many a time absorbing external traumas unknowingly and not giving themselves time to restore the disintegrated energies of their bodies and minds. Some even feel guilty to take a holiday when there is so much anguish and suffering going around in the world. The belief one can give more and more can make one feel invincible till a nervous or physical breakdown happens.

To give shade, a tree needs ample sunlight and nutrients to survive and grow tall. Likewise, all caregivers and empaths need to understand that their self-care is extremely necessary to be able to give the soothing shade they wish to provide.

Throughout this book I have highlighted, in different ways, the deep connection between mind, body and soul. Understanding this intense interconnectedness does help in identifying imbalances and disharmonies a little sooner than later. Awareness of how the body is reacting due to thoughts in the mind leads to a soul-satisfying or soul-disrupting life. You might not 'see' the ethereal soul, but you definitely feel it when you bump into your soulmate or twin flame, when you hear the heartbeat of your unborn child, when you feel cradled by a warm light in your meditation, when you hold a dying person's hand and tenderly aid the soul to cross over.

To connect or reconnect with one's authentic self, it is desired that one drops all artifice and unwanted judgements of the self and others. Ego-driven emotions don't have the capacity to give us much; they only distract us from our self-growth. When the ego rears its ugly head, water it down by remembering we *all* come from the same fountainhead of creation, and there aren't even six degrees of separation amongst us. We are more connected than disconnected, as some tend to preach.

And beware of the fake messiahs who tell you to follow their way as it is the only way to enlightenment, or the sweet-talking harbingers of doom who push humanity to fight, kill and conquer. Even the religious zealots who spew fire and brimstone about the burning fires of hell must be ignored. Heaven or hell is a state of mind that we create and that we have the power to un-create.

My dear friend Nikhat Bhatty is a spiritual healer, a writer of fiction, non-fiction and screenplays, and my partner in invigorating conversations about humanity, metaphysics and hyacinths for the soul.[1]

Always willing to heal and be healed, here is what Nikhat has to say:

'"Love is the only way there is ... Love is all there is ... You must forgive him, with love ..."

'I rejected that, of course. How was it even possible to forgive a betrayal so horrible, so painful? And with love? Excuse me, what rubbish! The betrayer was evil, unworthy of love. I mean, one has to draw a line somewhere, right? I must stand up for myself against the perpetrator of such evil! I might eventually forgive, but love? No chance! These thoughts raced about in my head as I felt myself sinking, falling headlong into a deep, dark abyss. And there I stayed and would have remained, had not those words that were ringing in my ears slowly descended into my heart—never deserting me, never abandoning me. They wrapped themselves around me with the same love they were advocating, till I learnt to hold on to them and used them as a rope to climb back up into the light again.

'I did forgive, with love. And felt free.

---

[1] This alludes to the poem 'Hyacinths to Feed Thy Soul' by the thirteenth-century Persian poet Muslihuddin Saadi.

'I didn't know then, but someone, somewhere was looking out for me and knew I was going to nosedive into that deep, dark abyss.

'But my path to "healing Nikhat" began when I forgot to carry any reading material on a flight to London. Bored of watching movies, I asked a colleague for a book, and she handed me *Many Lives, Many Masters* by Dr Brian Weiss. By the time I landed back home, I was hooked enough to buy some more of his books. And a read-through of the back of one of those books was a small hypnosis exercise. I tried it with a friend and found myself experiencing a past life. I saw my guide, Ra'tun, standing in the middle of a large room in a blue-tiled palace that had streaks of light streaming in through the windows, forming shimmery patterns on the floor.

'I was a little girl in rags, totally awestruck by my beautiful surroundings. I intuitively knew that this was not my home but that this tall, kind man standing in front of me was definitely someone of mine. I could not tear my eyes away from his beautiful, compassionate face! I experienced love of a kind that fills your heart and feels complete. But I couldn't place him in any recognizable way. He kept gazing at me with love, and I returned his gaze with love too. The read-through came to an end and my friend holding the session asked me to open my eyes. I did not want to. I did not want to leave this man's presence. But I opened my eyes and asked my friend, "Who was he?" And she replied, "The Bhatty, I haven't a clue!"

'From that day on, the clue became clear. I found that I could communicate with Ra'tun whenever I wanted. And he would speak to me. All I needed to do was close my eyes, tune out from the physical outer world and tune in to my inner world, with silence. Basically, meditate. And Ra'tun would gently, but firmly when required, answer all my questions about the happenings in my life. He made no predictions, just pointed a finger in the direction I needed to look. It was my choice to put one foot in front of the other and walk in that direction or not. I chose to do so. I believed in him. It was not possible for someone with such kind eyes to lead me astray. Also, I found peace in his guidance. Which was way better than how I was feeling with my eyes open, navigating my life! And slowly, a shift in my perspective, my belief system, started to take place. My difficult life seemed to become more bearable; my problems melted away.

'Every bit I write here is true. And as events unfolded, I lived that truth. And as I did that, my understanding about who I really am grew, and the most wonderful journey into myself manifested into existence an experience of a fabulous life filled with gratitude.

'So, what I learnt is that we create our experiences. Karma is real, and the universe is a force much stronger than our ego/will. Understanding karma and collaborating with the universe (which is really the CPU of divine intelligence) creates our experiences.

They are of our choosing and our own creation. What wonderful empowerment that is!

'But to make that journey into our self, we need help. I was guided to a living guru, but not everyone has that experience. In which case, everything that guides us towards help is our guru. Our minds are conditioned by the family we belong to, the society we live in and our individual experiences up to the point of awakening. These create a barrier/veil that obstructs the power of our true self. For the longest time, I believed that the universe was a horrible thing, against me most of the time, and try as hard as I did, I seemed to be swimming against the tide. And the strong force opposed to me was the universe itself! As I understood it then, the universe was something unknown, ominous and just mean. But unknown to me, the "mean universe" was hard at work, pushing me in a direction that I needed to flow into to realize my own power.

'Tired and in distress, it pushed me to discover hypnotherapy as a healing mechanism. Being in hypnosis connected me to that part of myself that was hidden behind the veil of my artificial self, my ego self—the self erected by the forces of the physical world I inhabited. It introduced me to the other world, equally real but invisible to the eye—the ethereal, intangible inner world or divine world. And it was there, with my eyes closed but heart and mind open, that I first met my spirit guide, Ra'tun. And thence started a fascinating journey that took me step by step into myself. Knowledge is empowerment, and once I was able to know why my current life was the way it was, I was able to consciously and deliberately, with hard inner work, change it into a better one, a life that was conscious and thriving. The start of that awareness came to me via hypnotherapy sessions.

'When I lost my mother, I felt lost. Not unhappy or sad for long but just empty. Directionless. That was when I asked Sabari to conduct a session for me. I needed to know which direction to go in. I wanted an LBL session, as I needed to understand where the crossroads I was on could lead to. So that I could consciously choose. Expecting and hoping to meet my mother in regression, I was surprised that once in that space beyond linear time, it didn't really matter to me. I saw her, acknowledged her, and there was an instant understanding that we would meet again and again, just as we have in the past, and that there is no separation at all. But in that session, so much else was also understood. Guided gently by Sabari, I learnt some of my soul's patterns that I needed to break in this life. The opportunities were there, but I had not been aware. There were patterns that had been coming along with me, coded into my spiritual DNA, so to say, that I had planned on shedding in this life. Since the time I became aware, it has been possible for me to slowly and consciously start that shedding process. Indeed, each time I have reached out and sought help,

I have shed with awareness some heaviness or the other—carried on my shoulders for lives and lives. Such freedom and lightness!

'But in the end, after all the sessions and inner work, it is still Ra'tun's words that ring true. Love is the answer. And the only way there is. And love begins by loving oneself. It is this that sets one off on a journey of self-discovery, so exciting and thrilling that as each layer of oneself is unravelled, the joy and love only increase. I wish all to have this experience, to feel loved and guided and walk with a piquant step towards self-awareness, as life can be as beautiful as you choose it to be.'

The path to finding the self quite often begins serendipitously. A stray comment from a stranger, a book someone asks you to read out of the blue, a film that you watch just to kill the time but that sets your mind afire, the lyrics of a song. There are so many ways the universe prepares us before we actually set foot on the path to self-realization. We might call them coincidences or accidents, but they happen as they are meant to happen. They are markers that your soul had decided in advance, while making the blueprint of a lifetime, to shine light on the amnesia of a human birth.

All these markers subtly nudge us towards spiritual experiences and explorations. My need to explore, to dig deeper beyond this one life, started seriously after reading *Many Lives, Many Masters*, when I had just started high school. Already exposed to Hindu mythological stories and the Indian epics the Ramayana and the Mahabharata, my mind was open to the concepts of 'beyond life' and the afterlife. So *Many Lives, Many Masters* sealed the deal, and my old soul in a young body wanted to investigate space, time and eternity.

When a call or a calling comes, try not to ignore it. Keep your heart and mind open, for you never know what magical adventure it might lead you to. For example, if you chance upon a picture of or a quote from a divine guru and your heart cries out to connect with the guru, allow yourself to feel the connection physically and metaphysically. Who knows, the guru might have been waiting for you for a couple of lifetimes. If you do not answer your heart's call, you will not know it, will you?

You embody the past, the present is a gift and you are continuously creating your future through kriya (deeds) and karma (results of the deeds). The energy that you are, you are doing so much work to experience the myriad shades of maya in the varying schools you choose to go to. We must understand and integrate all our shadows holistically, keep the mind-body connection harmonious and nourish our spiritual self too. Living is not a very easy business on planet Earth, as this school can get quite tough if we choose to ignore our lessons and not learn from them.

I have said many times: The questions and the answers both lie within ourselves. Only when the veils around our true selves are lifted layer by layer do we manage to reach the answers to our questions. Once the extraneous baggage surrounding us is surrendered into the light of healing, we truly break free from the shackles around our soul and then start enjoying the joy of living in all its glory.

Chapter 10
Self-Help Tools and Reading List

'And above all, watch with glittering eyes the whole world around you because the greatest secrets are always hidden in the most unlikely places. Those who don't believe in magic will never find it.'

— **Roald Dahl**

In my own serendipitous path to spiritual knowledge and healing, I was steered by my guides and my own higher self. We are all guided similarly, if we care to listen, and often we get to sip the elixir for living well.

My soul mien is that of an explorer, a researcher of words and worlds, infinitely hungry for all experiences. Especially experiences that help me grow and feel like a warm hug. My love of world mythology was sown by my storytelling grandparents. My maternal grandmother did not live in my city, but whenever we visited each other, I heard stories too. She was an ardent Lord Krishna devotee, and she narrated beautiful, vivid stories of the boy with a peacock feather tucked in his bandana who played the flute so mesmerizingly.

I do not know if the stories, simply and unknowingly, prepared me for the vagaries of life that were to surface soon enough, but what they did without a doubt is give me an unshakeable faith in magic.

Magic exists everywhere, in and around us. The moment we orient ourselves to be open to magic, we start receiving healthy sprinklings of magic dust, and some fairy and pixie dust as well. All this tinsel shows up as interesting gurus, wise teachers and soul-lifting experiences, and gives us a chance to delve into transcendent creativity, which has been gifted to the world by mystical artists.

I threw myself into understanding the esoteric world through copious amounts of reading.

The intense reading was possible because of my mother. She was the assistant librarian at the National Library of India, Kolkata, and I used her position to access the rarest books from the stacks and read in the huge main reading room. The old edifice that houses the main reading room was the designated home for all the Governor-Generals of the East India Company, who had their headquarters in Kolkata (then Calcutta). The main reading room was the ballroom in those days, and it had high, cavernous ceilings, tall glass windows and a beautifully polished wooden floor. In an erstwhile ballroom of the British Raj began my forays into understanding the esoteric and occult world.

Here is a list of some of the fascinating books I read in my early days of exploration, which I recommend you read to open your mind.

- *Metamorphoses* by Ovid
- Greek and Roman mythology books, which included Homer's *The Odyssey*
- The Mahabharata
- The Ramayana
- The Jataka tales
- Miscellaneous tales from the Puranas
- Cheiro's books on palmistry and other astrological books
- *God Speaks* by Meher Baba
- *Autobiography of a Yogi* by Yogananda
- Some of Bhagwan Rajneesh's conversations in his many books and audio recordings. A good start to understanding his teachings is to read *Meditation for Busy People*
- *The World According to Garp* by John Irving, one of my favourite writers

I would urge you to read all of Brian Weiss's books if you feel a keen interest in knowing deeply about reincarnation and the concept of soul journeys.

Another groundbreaking book on the subject is *Where Reincarnation and Biology Intersect* by Ian Stevenson.

Nan Umrigar's *Sounds of Silence: A Bridge Across Two Worlds* is an intensely personal book about a feted young jockey, Karl Umrigar, who died in an accident at the Mahalaxmi Racecourse in Mumbai. Karl connected with his mother, Nan, from the spirit world through automatic writing, revealing that he was under the guidance of Avatar Meher Baba. Magically, I got the opportunity to connect with Nan Umrigar, and through her facilitation, I too was led to Meher Baba, my spiritual guru over lifetimes.

When I read Michael Newton's first book, *Journey of Souls*, my soul song was blaring and a pleasurable tingle of anticipation kept me glued to the book, reading case study after case study that talked about a loving place vibrating to soothing frequencies of harmonious energies: 'Heaven', which we don't know in Earth school, but where we surely belong as spiritual beings. This is one of the best books on the afterlife, and it is filled with astounding details of the afterlife that need to be read to be believed.

Michael Newton's second book, *Destiny of Souls*, delves deeper into the afterlife, with more information on the spirit world.

Books speak to us. While browsing in a bookshop or online, a particular book might immediately grab our attention and we just cannot ignore it, even if we pass it by—we are pulled back to it again. That's the book you need to buy. It's seeking your attention because it has something to offer you, and your higher consciousness has picked it up. This randomness keeps happening to me all the time, and I am the one who gains at the end of it.

Linda Goodman is well known as an astrologer, and her books *Love Signs* and *Sun Signs* have had phenomenal sales globally. But what most people do not know is that Goodman is a psychic and a practitioner of the Jewish Kabbalah system of numerology. Her book *Star Signs*, which I first read in 1989, is still my go-to book when I want a perk-up read on the occult and other related subjects, like the concepts of twin flames and twin souls

All of Deepak Chopra's books. His books appeal to me because he writes on profound things with a certain lightness—without any pompousness—and that is what touches the heart and is carried within. His book *The Seven Spiritual Laws of Success*, in a way, saved me from going crazy during the painful unspooling of my first marriage. I had bought the book on a whim, and it used to be on my office desk at the advertising agency where I worked then. To hold it together, especially after disturbing phone calls from the then-husband, I would automatically open the book and start reading. Garbled sentences would slowly straighten out and eventually make sense. Deep exhalations and Chopra's wise words would slowly calm my nerves and I would relax. I read this book so many times during that period. Unbeknownst to Deepak Chopra, his book threw me a line to hold on to when I was drowning.

Follow your instinct and plunge into the words of all the prophets of light and absorb the luminosity of knowledge.

Mind and body well-being

As the mind and soul are getting nurtured, keep a tab on how the physical body is feeling. The body is the channel through which everything passes, so it's important to take care of it.

Practise cleanliness, regular exercise, yoga and tai chi for a peaceful balance between mind and body.

Many people go to attend yoga workshops in nature, mindfulness workshops, soul-healing workshops, etc. My advice would be to put yourself out there and see what works for you. When some offering for the expansion of the self clicks, then it's magic all over again.

Wanderlust and pixie dust are a heady combination and can get you hooked for life. Travel and see the planet you inhabit. Go without any preconceptions and absorb everything like a sponge. My travels have taught me beautiful lessons, where I have just followed my heart and allowed myself to be guided divinely. Rubbing shoulders with different civilizations with different codes of conduct and different ways to love has taught me that we are all the same. We come from the same fountainhead of universal energy and are woven together with limitless love. Turn your gaze inward, and with your inner vision, recognize this connection through space and time.

On all self-journeys of seeking, we need to learn to be a little vulnerable. Vulnerability is not necessarily disadvantageous if it comes from a place of quiet strength. I see and meet so many people who feel impaired by the thought of emotional intimacy. Maybe they are not scared of new love or intimate relationships but have a fear born of old wounds. Old traumas, especially emotional traumas arising from rejection, tend to paralyze the ability to be vulnerable. One is always checking on the walls they have built for protection and choosing to live half a life behind those walls. It takes courage to break those walls, but trust me, when you choose to heal and break free from old traumas, you are giving yourself the gift of a magnificent future. I too had to crawl out from behind so many walls and boundaries I had built so that I could walk towards the light.

There is an array of wonderful tools of healing out there. I seized them all. I plunged my senses into the performing arts, painted my heart out, watched the frequency of God's light lighting up a mountain top and clicked the shutter of my camera with awe, danced through moonlit nights and watched the sun come up on a pink horizon. I meditated deeply, sometimes unable to even feel my physical body, and sometimes I struggled to keep my attention on one thing. But I fought and smashed my way out through the fog to be the best I can be.

You can do it too if you wish to. Live, breathe, heal and find your own serendipitous path to your magic and healing.

Inner child work helped me a lot in shedding my emotional baggage and being freer.

I also benefitted immensely from sound healing. Trained practitioners use big Tibetan gongs and bowls of various sizes, and when they 'play' these instruments with a wooden stick, the vibrations roll through the various chakras and energy centres in the body, opening up blocks.

Dr Evelet Sequeira in Mumbai is a fabulous life coach and experienced sound healer. Here is what she has written for you, giving you all a deeper understanding of sound healing.

What is sound healing?

Sound healing is a practice that uses relaxing sound vibrations produced by the human vocals or voice and instruments like Tibetan singing bowls, tuning forks, gongs, etc., to promote relaxation and stimulate healing by affecting one's physiology, neurology and psychology. A sound therapist is a person who is trained in the use of sound healing methods and uses a holistic approach in order to restore balance to an individual's energy field at the physical, emotional, mental and spiritual level using various sound therapy instruments.

How does sound healing affect the physical body?

Deep relaxation: Various studies have proven that sound waves with frequencies between 4 and 10 hertz create theta and alpha brainwaves, which, in turn, induce deep meditative states.[1] Studies and clinical observations by Dr Mitchell

---

[1] Jorge Vera, Ulises Pereira, Bryan Reynaert, Juan Bacigalupo, Magdalena Sanhueza, 'Neuronal resonance in the theta (4-10 Hz) frequency range is modulated by dynamic changes in the input resistance', https://www.biorxiv.org/content/10.1101/224253v1.full

Gaynor suggest that sound interventions elicit the 'relaxation response' of the nervous system.[2] The sound of Tibetan bowls, gongs and vocal toning can alter these brainwaves and thus calm the mind and induce a state of psychophysical relaxation.

Evokes an emotional response: Sound therapy using various instruments can evoke an emotional response in those clients whose nervous system is in a frozen state due to stress or trauma. Sound is a powerful vehicle for emotional healing, as different types of music evoke different emotional states.

Frequency + intention = healing: This equation, given by noted sound healer Jonathan Goldman, speaks of intention as the energy behind a sound. The consciousness of the intention travels with the sound and brings about physical healing. Sound delivered at a proper frequency and vibrational intensity can heal at the cellular level, as investigated by Dr Jeffrey Thompson, DC, Director, Center for Neuroacoustic Research, California.[3]

---

[2] Mitchell L. Gaynor MD, *The healing power of sound* (Shambala, 13 August 2002).

[3] Jonathan Goldman, *The 7 secrets of sound healing* (Hay House, 2008).

Harmonizes cells: Vocal toning is the use of one's own voice to produce vowel sounds. This is done on an elongated outbreath. It increases oxygenations of the cells and releases endorphins, which are self-created opiates, to recover from chronic painful conditions. It also stimulates cells to produce nitric oxide, a vasodilator that opens up blood vessels.

Immune system: It was seen that frequencies between 40 and 115 hertz diminished hematic cortisol concentration in 86 per cent of those tested.[4] Sound increases antibody production for better immunity, helps decrease cortisol and increases lymphatic circulation.

Sleep quality: Sound baths can help increase melatonin production, improve sleep quality and reduce insomnia symptoms. After a sound bath, people have experienced deep, restorative sleep.

---

[4] Tamara L Goldsby et al, 'Effects of singing bowl sound meditation on mood, tension, and well-being: An observational study', Complementary Altern Med 30 September 2016.

The universe is offering us so many tools for healing and rejuvenation. All we have to do is explore with an open mind and receive the gifts that will enhance our growth.

I would like to leave you with a passage from Linda Goodman's *Star Signs*. I have read this passage many times over, through sorrow and joy, through the depths of gloom and through soaring happiness. It has never disappointed me, and it always gives me perspective in every situation.

> in some silent depths I feel mysteriously drawn
> to probe
> for lost Essenic pearls of truth
>
> which first appear, then disappear
> in swirls of deep green water
>
> wisps of love ... hazes of fear
> sometimes distorted ... sometimes clear
>
> and always the question
> why?
>
> what is this insistent pull on my mind?
> what is it urging me to find?
> is it simply a need to pursue, with Aries persistence
> the reason for humanity's continued existence?

no, I fear it is something more ... long lost on a forgotten shore
calling me on and on ... to explore ... the ancient laws
of Karma.

Masks

There is no shame in being naked.
Being vulnerable without a hundred veils.

There is shame in hiding behind masks.
In not engaging or receiving the world with deep honesty.

There is shame in not being you through fear or guilt or guile.

Freedom, love, passion, truth are not just nice words.
They hold the key to our salvation.

Note to self: Be fearless and free ♥

I wrote this on 22 June 2019, blissfully unaware that very soon we would have to wear masks to save our lives. Madame Irony must have had a lopsided smirk when I was writing this. The world plunged into darkness, flapped around hopelessly and then finally found an anchor in 'healing', both the self and others. Nature healed itself, the ozone layer around the Earth effortlessly repaired its cracks and people joined meditation and restorative groups for their mental, physical and emotional well-being. Quietly the light spread and obliterated the darkness. We eternal beings of energy broke free from our shackles and embraced healing, enhanced our vibrations positively, opened our hearts, gave and received love. Some of us also touched the unlimited potential within our true selves and finally understood the meaning of 'Aham Brahmasmi'—I am divine.

> *'Follow your bliss and the universe will open doors where there were only walls.'*
> —**Joseph Campbell**

Acknowledgements

There are so many souls to acknowledge—people and animals. My life has been shaped by multitudinous experiences, some of which have broken and smashed me to such an extent that I have actively craved sweet, obliterating darkness. But then I learnt to rise from the ashes and shine like the proverbial phoenix.

There are so many friends to thank who never let go of my hand. The list is too long, but as you read these words, you know who you are.

I have also had uplifting, exhilarating experiences that have always kept the 'renaissance of wonder' within me alive and have never choked my laughter. My earliest partner in crime was the very first friend I ever made in my childhood, Rinku, now departed from this earth, who never said no to me, never judged me and loved me completely.

My dearest school friend, Farida Bootwala, who succumbed to cancer and left us physically—I love her and miss her so much. She taught me again how to give love selflessly.

For this book, I wish to thank the maverick Kanishka Gupta, the best literary agent an author could desire. Kanishka, himself very intuitive and gifted, convinced me to write this book, and here I am. We are friends and I am happy he is in my life.

Trisha Bora, my editor at HarperCollins India, should be given a Nobel Prize for patience. I fell severely ill between 2021 and 2023, and there were long gaps when I could not sit down to write, but Trisha never gave up on me. She believed in this book with all her heart and kept encouraging me to finish the manuscript when I was ready to give up. I hugely appreciate her suggestions and never-ending forbearance.

My gangs of women friends from middle school, high school, college and different workplaces, I want you to know that your loving friendship fills me with joie de vivre and I draw so much sustenance from you rocking women.

My guides and masters, especially my guru, Meher Baba, who spiritually mentors me in everything I do. His physical body is no more on earth, but his ethereal presence always embraces me in silence and in talk. This relationship cannot be described. Only felt.

Lord Shiva, who knows it all—destruction, forgiveness, creation—to whom I surrender from my soul with all-encompassing gratitude. I seek blessings from this vibration, the Adiguru of all healing, and I am always infinitely blessed.

All my teachers from whom I learnt therapeutic and healing practices. You gave from your heart, which I received in my heart. I will remain forever obliged for the sacred knowledge you shared.

My husband and my four-legged children hold everything together for me, and without their love and conviction that 'Mama is the strongest', sometimes I might have blinked first. They are my strength and loving beings of light with whom I have the most fun.

Love and thankfulness to all the people who hurt me deeply, who abandoned me, who lied in my name but made me believe they were friends. I chose you from my soul group to teach me hard lessons through which I would learn and grow spiritually. You played your role only because I had asked you to do me wrong in my human avatar. It must have hurt you deep within, but you agreed to play along so I grew. You *are* my soul friends in the spirit world, and I bless you.

To each one of you radiant beams of sunshine who loved and protected me and flickered and flitted in and out of my life, I can only say my soul understood your soul song and we made celestial music here on earth.

I feel blessed to have had the greatest teachers and mentors while training in PLR therapy with Dr Brian Weiss and clinical hypnotherapy as well as the LBL spiritual regression programme at the Michael Newton

Institute. They have taught me, trusted me, inspired me and guided me. I have also learnt inner child therapy, emotional freedom technique (EFT), Usui reiki and metaphor therapy. Each of these has helped me create my own integrated approach to healing with some very positive results. I have also been an LBL training instructor, a case reviewer and a mentor with the Michael Newton Institute.

My spirit guides and masters from the spirit world made my journey and this book possible. I am blessed to have finely honed my extrasensory perception (ESP), and my guides have whispered and hollered (when needed) their spiritual guidance every time I have sought it. My guides joined many dots for me when I was blind and never once abandoned me in this wilderness called life.

Last but not the least, thank you, HarperCollins India, for holding space while I wrote *Break Free*.

About the Author

Sabari Chakraborty is a past life regression therapist trained and certified by Dr Brian Weiss, bestselling author of *Many Lives, Many Masters*. She is also an Integrated Clinical Hypnotherapist trained and certified by the California Hypnosis Institute of India (Mumbai). She is also a Life Between Lives (LBL) regression therapist, the first in India, and has been trained and certified by the Michael Newton Institute in the US. She has undergone teachers training in LBL therapy at the Michael Newton Institute.

In her integrated healing practice, she uses Inner Child Therapy (trained by Trisha Caetano), EFT (trained by Dr Paula Horan) and Metaphor Therapy (working with visual and verbal metaphors). Sabari is also an Usui Reiki practitioner and a lifelong student of Vedic astrology.

HarperCollins *Publishers* India

At HarperCollins India, we believe in telling the best stories and finding the widest readership for our books in every format possible. We started publishing in 1992; a great deal has changed since then, but what has remained constant is the passion with which our authors write their books, the love with which readers receive them, and the sheer joy and excitement that we as publishers feel in being a part of the publishing process.

Over the years, we've had the pleasure of publishing some of the finest writing from the subcontinent and around the world, including several award-winning titles and some of the biggest bestsellers in India's publishing history. But nothing has meant more to us than the fact that millions of people have read the books we published, and that somewhere, a book of ours might have made a difference.

As we look to the future, we go back to that one word—a word which has been a driving force for us all these years.

Read.